Praise for *Soul Food*

"Established by Tilden Edwards those many years ago the Shalem Institute has continued to offer a safe space for individuals to engage with the sacred and restore the divine image, loving God. An illuminating addition is a testament to the institute's rich history contemplative spiritual growth."

—author of *Falling Upward*
and founder of the Center for Action and Contemplation

"Exploring numerous rich perspectives on contemporary Christianity—from gender identity and theological languaging to issues of recovery, welcome and inclusion, decolonization, and social action, among others—the authors are unafraid to tackle new perspectives, all the while staying firmly rooted in the core of their faith. Anyone interested in immersing themselves in these topics will be well served here."

**—Rev. SeiFu Singh-Molares,
Executive Director of Spiritual Directors International**

"With this book, Shalem sets forth a radical agenda for the next fifty years where we must do all we can to bend the arc of the moral universe toward love, truth, and justice. If you have any affinity for the contemplative life, you'll find this book a compelling companion as we work and pray for the Beloved Community."

**—Parker J. Palmer, author of *Let Your Life Speak*,
The Courage to Teach, and *On the Brink of Everything*,
and founder of the Center for Courage & Renewal**

"*Soul Food* is a community of contemplative authors also compassionately addressing the ailments of our society. Their work offers us new wineskins of openheartedness, which can help us create a larger table where everyone is invited to sit and have plenty. It invites all to savor Love, 'the [Ancient] New,' and it gives us contemplative ways to do that in a world of collective and personal trauma."

**—Carmen Acevedo Butcher, PhD, poet,
and translator of *Practice of the Presence*
and *The Cloud of Unknowing***

"Today, if there is one word that says what our human family most urgently needs to recover, awe is that word. Experiencing awe makes us one. Awe is the magic wand that can transform I-thinking into We-thinking and rescue us from self-destruction. That *Soul Food* devotes so much space to awe honors Shalem's finest tradition and makes it a most timely book of hope for the world."
—**Br. David Steindl-Rast, Benedictine monk, author, and co-founder of Grateful Living**

"*Soul Food* is a worthy guide for those who seek to walk in the light and share that light with others. Thoughtful and engaging on many levels, it is indeed a nourishing book."
—**Sophfronia Scott, author of** *The Seeker and the Monk: Everyday Conversations with Thomas Merton*

"This celebratory volume for the Shalem Institute marks a rich history of leadership in spiritual formation by offering challenging and visionary reflection on the future of contemplation. The feast offered is varied, rich, and engaging—some of it stimulating, some soothing, all providing much-needed nourishment that defies ready categorization, except for its quality. This is a further gift to all who have benefitted from the work of Shalem, and all who should."
—**The Very Rev. Dr. Andrew McGowan, Dean and President, Berkeley Divinity School, and McFaddin Professor of Anglican Studies, Yale Divinity School**

"For an everyday, this-worldly perspective on contemplative life and leadership, read *Soul Food*. Any one of the essays will be worth the whole book."
—**Keith Kristich, meditation teacher and founder of the online, interspiritual community Closer Than Breath**

"*Soul Food* demonstrates that the life of prayer and contemplation is never detached from the urgent issues of the day, reminding us that the foundation of the spiritual life is all about contemplation and leadership. These essays will make you pray, think, see, act, and live differently. Their voices are the tongues of fire calling us into a new experience of Pentecost and sacred living."
—**The Rev. Dr. Mark Francisco Bozzuti-Jones, Priest, author of** *Absalom Jones* **and** *Face to the Rising Sun*, **and Director of Spiritual Formation at Trinity Retreat Center**

SOUL FOOD

Nourishing Essays on Contemplative
Living and Leadership

Edited by Westina Matthews, Margaret Benefiel,
and Jackson Droney

Church Publishing
NEW YORK

Scripture quotations marked (NRSV) are from New Revised Standard Version Bible, copyright © 1989 National Council of the Churches of Christ in the United States of America. Used by permission. All rights reserved worldwide.

Scripture quotations marked (NIV) are taken from the Holy Bible, New International Version®, NIV®. Copyright © 1973, 1978, 1984, 2011 by Biblica, Inc.™ Used by permission of Zondervan. All rights reserved worldwide. www.zondervan.com. The "NIV" and "New International Version" are trademarks registered in the United States Patent and Trademark Office by Biblica, Inc.™

Scripture quotations marked (NKJV) are taken from the New King James Version®. Copyright © 1982 by Thomas Nelson. Used by permission. All rights reserved.

Scripture quotations marked (NJB) are taken from The New Jerusalem Bible, published and copyright 1985 by Darton, Longman & Todd Ltd and Les Editions du Cerf, and used by permission of the publishers.

Scripture quotations marked (ESV) are from The ESV® Bible (The Holy Bible, English Standard Version®), copyright © 2001 by Crossway, a publishing ministry of Good News Publishers. Used by permission. All rights reserved."

Church Publishing
19 East 34th Street
New York, NY 10016

Cover art: iStockphoto.com / Silmen / Stock illustration ID:180691632
Typeset by Nord Compo

A record of this book is available from the Library of Congress.

ISBN 978-1-64065-634-5 (paperback)
ISBN 978-1-64065-635-2 (ebook)

To the Rev. Dr. Tilden H. Edwards
Shalem's beloved founder and senior fellow

Contents

Part 1
Welcoming and Belonging

Part 2
Holy Awe

Foreword

Valerie Brown

was raised by womenfolk, my mother and her three sisters, and my grandmother, who all loved to cook soul food. Sundays growing up in Brooklyn were not just for Mass at the local Catholic church; they were the time when my mother and all the women got together to cook Jamaican dishes adapted to America. Stewed oxtail with black-eyed peas and rice, corn bread, and collard greens not only nourished my hunger, but they also sustained my soul that was worn weary by violence, poverty, and injustice. Being in the kitchen with these women was a respite, a place of utter transparency. In other words, it was a place of love, belonging, and connectedness. During the longest part of these Sundays cooking together, the part that I savored even more than the food, was the sense of hospitality, the listening presence, and attentiveness that saturated each moment.

While the struggle and turbulence, the injustices, oppression, and discrimination were still there, not far away, these Sundays felt infused with prayerful awareness, tenderness, and joy that offered subsistence, courage, and direction. Those days prepared me so well for a life of leadership and contemplation, though I didn't know it back then. The flavor of those Sunday meal gatherings is echoed in the pages of this book: how to lead, love, create; how to steward this land and each other; how to nurture a living encounter with God, Spirit.

The wisdom of this book is nourishment for the soul, offering inspiration for those who lead and for those who aspire to lead, for those who seek to live with greater intentionality, integrity, purpose, connection, and compassion. This collection of our stories feels very much like chatting around the kitchen table. Our stories are food, nourishment, pouring through our hands, supporting each other toward greater liberating awareness, greater wholeness.

The first half of the collection, "Welcoming and Belonging," offers individual and collective wanderings within systems and structures of oppression, and brave acts of decolonizing forms of spiritual companioning and spiritual direction that begin with unpacking the words we choose to describe God, who teaches what, and how. *Soul Food* lifts up the voice of Black biblical scholarship, which too often is sidelined, made invisible by systems of patriarchy. The truth-telling here naturally invites big questions, such as what is at stake when spiritual companioning programs delink social context from praxis? Do these programs uphold dominant spiritual norms and, by omission, explicitly or implicitly continue to marginalize underrepresented voices? How do we bring gender-inclusive language and thought into the teaching of spiritual formation programs and curriculum? We can do better. We will do better, and these chapters offer a vision forward.

These are stories of our luminous natural world as teacher and guide, reminding us that, ultimately, awe and wonder are available each moment, never far away or out of reach. They shine light on interconnectedness and interbeing. We are not separate, isolated from the intricate web of the living cosmos of plants, animals, minerals, oceans, and forests. We belong to the natural world as to each other. Through small circles, in community, we learn belonging and welcoming, learning to listen with the whole body, the heart, the eyes, the ears, and the mind, and to be in resonance with each other as a foundation for vitality and vulnerability.

In part 2 of *Soul Food* we turn to Holy Awe, which opens with a chapter on the many ways to know God's presence, to find peace within, and to share that with others. Whether we choose centering prayer or silence, a walk at sunset or ecstatic dance, our authentic expression is invited forward. The breath, slow and deep, is prayer.

Focusing on embodied leadership, another chapter offers the compelling story and liberating spirituality of Howard Thurman, often considered the godfather of the civil rights movement and one of the most influential spiritual leaders of the twentieth century, in a portrait of Thurman's commitment to shared unity, nonviolence, and contemplation to advance social change. Using the metaphor of pilgrimage, we relearn the power of spiritual resilience through the act of travel to a sacred place for a sacred purpose. And through the aging process with grace and resilience, we become more available to experience our work as generative and joyful, asking: What are my gifts and how can I be of service?

The language of Holy Awe is love that is rediscovered when people gather to reconnect to the felt sense of belonging through undefended conversations and receptive hearts that are animated through true connection. The lingering taste that remains for me with *Soul Food* is a sense of true refuge, of peace illuminated by the stories of many spiritual paths and practices, and a call to social engagement toward social justice and peace. In recognition of the importance of Shalem's founding fifty years ago, this is the time not just to look back at the lives touched and leaders transformed but also to look ahead to the next fifty years of ministry expanded by a vision of Beloved Community rooted in compassionate action, justice, peace, and love.

Valerie Brown
New Hope, Pennsylvania
April 27, 2023

A Note from the Founder
Tilden Edwards

Fifty years ago, at the founding of Shalem, we envisioned a place for contemplative prayer, a place of awe and wonder. We knew that Shalem's life was ultimately a holy mystery. We could probe that mystery by leaning back into God's loving presence and being open to what might be given us as we asked to be shown what was ours to know and do that could take us the next step toward that vision. We could seek to trust that whatever we would know and do would be grounded in love, faith, and in an open-ended hope that ultimately was beyond our full comprehension. We brought an open-minded/open-hearted listening stance to all that we did.

Shalem's history shows us the great value of forming small groups for reflection on our spiritual lives, where we begin each group in silence, and return to that silence as needed. In that silence we have opportunity to ground ourselves in our spiritual hearts, deeper than our minds and egos. Collectively, then, we find ourselves relating to one another on a more intimate, heart-to-heart level.

Now, fifty years later, I find myself amazed at what God has done through Shalem. While Shalem's life still remains a holy mystery, ultimately there is a shimmering golden thread of how contemplative living and leadership have been manifested at Shalem over the decades. Now, with six long-term programs, as well as short-term programs, pilgrimages, and online courses, we continue to experience the gift of grounding ourselves in our spiritual hearts. Small groups continue to be at the core of Shalem programs and at the core of the Shalem society. In addition, with a board and staff committed to listening through leaning back into God's loving presence, decisions are made through a process of open-hearted discernment. It is out of this open-hearted listening to the Spirit that Vision 2025 emerged.

As Shalem moves into the future, we embrace Vision 2025 for the particular work that God has called us to in this time and place, as best as we can discern it. At the same time, we hold all of this lightly in the larger context of that holy mystery we call God. We will keep listening and keep seeking God's guidance even as we place one foot in front of another, following the illumination we have been given.

I look forward to seeing how God will manifest Vision 2025 at Shalem. It is important work that Shalem is called to do at this time.

Introduction

On the cusp of our fiftieth anniversary, as the Shalem Institute for Spiritual Formation continues to broaden our reach globally, we find that there are insufficient published resources that can speak from different perspectives on contemplative living and leadership in everyday life. To address this need, we have created *Soul Food*, an inclusive collection of essays on contemporary contemplative living and leadership. In 2022, we invited the over 5,000 Shalem graduates as well as current and previous Shalem board members and program directors to consider submitting essays for possible inclusion in this book. We intentionally sought a diverse group of contributors, including the LGBTQ+ community and people of all ethnicities and nationalities. From sixty essays submitted, we have selected seventeen to be included in this book. This collection of experiential and academic essays offers modern contemplative reflections from new and renowned voices.

We believe that there is Divine Diversity in our world, and we encourage you to be open to the endless possibilities. As such, the book is divided into two parts. The first is *Welcoming and Belonging*, in which one is invited to come to see God as other than who we may have traditionally known. The second is *Holy Awe*. You are invited to consider a variety of ways shared to shape your own practices of contemplative living and leadership.

Soul Food is intended not only for Shalem graduates but also for a wide range of audiences: participants in Shalem programs and pilgrimages, participants in other contemplative spiritual programs and organizations, students and faculty of seminaries and higher education institutions, spiritual communities and retreat centers, and seekers. It is our intent to support others in nourishing souls so that people can lead contemplative lives and offer leadership. We also believe that it is important to hear new voices to support those who are serving in a world that needs leaders trained to be deeply grounded, spiritually courageous, and ready to lead to transformation.

We are deeply indebted to our founder Tilden Edwards (for whom this book is dedicated). Many of us also remember Gerald G. "Jerry" May (1940–2005), a psychiatrist and author, and Rose Mary Doughtery, SNND (1936–2021), a teacher and author who shared their gifts as senior fellows. Their legacy is the springboard for the continuation of our deep commitment to contemplative living and leadership.

We also are committed to thinking expansively as we plan for the Shalem of the future, the Shalem that is becoming. Our vision for Shalem is that in 2025, Shalem will be a dynamic and inclusive community, empowered by the Spirit, where seekers engage in transformation of themselves, their communities, and the world through spiritual growth, deep connection, and courageous action. Shalem's Vision 2025 can be found at the end of this book. *Soul Food* is one step in realizing this vision.

At Shalem, we say, "We're seeking to live the contemplative life" or "We are contemplatives." But perhaps we might also ask ourselves, "Who is the 'we'?" Working and reflecting on the "we" is Shalem's ongoing commitment. The Divine Source invites all of us to draw on that Deep Well of Love. Now is the time to say "Yes!" to that invitation and to broaden the traditional understanding of what it means to be a contemplative leader in a diverse world.

In 1973 a young Episcopal priest, Rev. Dr. Tilden Edwards, felt drawn by a new call, a new vision of a deeper contemplative life in God for himself and for the world. Others who shared this vision joined with him, and the Shalem Institute for Spiritual Formation was born. Over the past fifty years, Shalem has grown in wisdom and grace, becoming a bright star in the constellation of organizations that promote and invite people into contemplative life and leadership. Thousands of like-spirited people from all over the world, drawn by the same call and vision, have participated in many and varied spiritual formation programs created by Shalem, extending its reach far beyond what that small group of seekers could have imagined.

Fifty years later the journey continues. We look ahead with great hope to a future shimmering with possibilities, revealing ever new ways of inviting even more seekers into our shared vision of a world transformed through contemplative life and leadership, abiding in the Great Love as one Beloved Community.

Westina Matthews, Margaret Benefiel, and Jackson Droney

Led by Starlight Down a Marvelous Road[1]

Winston Breeden Charles

The tree stands tall and broad beside the stream of living
water,
   abundant with fruit of all kinds:
      peaches and pears, nuts and nests,
         where birds learn to sing and fly.

So many walk by without seeing, so beyond wondrous it is—
   too preposterous to be perceived by mind's eye alone.

Perception requires the mind as it thinks, the heart as it feels,
   the body as it senses
   holy communion with the great love that blossoms here.

Tunnel vision breaks open into spacious wonder as choirs of
witnesses
   chant this deep reality residing at the heart of all.

Wisdom leads them by a marvelous road,[2]
   sheltering them by day,

---

1. In celebration of the fiftieth anniversary of the founding of the Shalem Institute for Spiritual Formation, January 2023.

2. Wisdom led them by a marvelous road; she herself was their shelter by day and their starlight through the night (Wisdom 10:17, NJB).

guiding them by starlight through the night,
faithfully holding them as they learn to fly.

Journeying with ongoing hope,
    abiding in the Great Love,
        drinking deeply of the life-giving water,
           sharing with others,
the great reveal unfolds into fullness of life and love.

Part 1
Welcoming and Belonging

At Shalem, we welcome everyone as they are, providing a safe and sacred space to explore on one's personal inward journey and serving as spiritual companions along the way. Or, as Ram Dass so eloquently reminded us, "We're all just walking each other home."[1] And along this walk, we are invited to not only welcome everyone but also to create a space for belonging.

Who do you welcome easily into your life? Are there perhaps people in your life that you use as foils for belonging? Are there people who because of their political ideology or life story or whose personal circumstances you judge morally? On the other hand, do you struggle to believe that you belong because you are different enough or have heard offhand comments enough, or have received body language enough times to tell you that "You're not one of us"?

As he traveled throughout the country, Martin Luther King Jr. often shared his own perspective on welcoming and belonging, and his understanding of the interrelatedness of the world:

> [All persons] are caught in an inescapable network of mutuality, tied in a single garment of destiny. Whatever affects one directly affects all indirectly. . . . I can never be what I ought to be until you are what you ought to be, and you can never be what you

---

1. "Ram Dass Quotes," Ram Dass Foundation, accessed March 23, 2023 https://www .ramdass.org/ram-dass-quotes/#more-13098.

ought to be until I am what I ought to be. This is the interrelated structure of reality.[2]

In the following collection of essays, the authors share their own experiences of welcoming and belonging, challenging us to expand our own understanding of the interrelatedness of the world. We begin with "God's Pronouns" by Carl McColman, in which he discusses how gendered pronouns unavoidably say something about our image and view of God and shares his own experience with gender identity.

---

2. "Dr. King's Words at MHC Inspire More than Fifty Years Later," Mount Holyoke Alumni Association, accessed March 23, 2023, https://alumnae.mtholyoke.edu/blog/dr-kings-words-at-mhc-inspire-50-years-later/.

1

God's Pronouns

A New Translation
of a Mystical Classic Invites Us
into the Beautiful Mystery of Gender

Carl McColman

few years ago, an editor I've often worked with asked
me if I would like to try my hand at translating. He was
hoping to publish a new edition of *The Cloud of Unknow-ing* and thought that I might be the right person for the task. I've
enjoyed reading *The Cloud* and the writings of Julian of Norwich
in the original Middle English, so this sounded like a wonderful
project to take on. I prayed about it and sat down to the computer
to try it out.

I didn't make it past the second page.

Translation is hard. It's far more difficult than simply following
one's inner muse to write something new. A good translation must
be faithful to its source material but also clear and understandable
while conveying the literary beauty and poetic rhythm of the orig-inal. As I struggled to balance these competing demands, I quickly
realized it takes a special kind of gift to translate well—and alas,
this was not my particular gift. My editor and I went on to another
idea, leaving me with a profoundly deepened sense of appreciation
and respect for the skill of good translators.

One such brilliant translator is Carmen Acevedo Butcher, whose own version of *The Cloud of Unknowing*[1] sets the bar so high that it is no wonder I felt unequal to the task. Her work is intimately faithful to the author's medieval voice, filled with spiritual earnest but also a sly sense of humor. There have been numerous modern English translations of *The Cloud* over the years, but I keep going back to the Acevedo Butcher translation, both for serious study and also devotional reading. If someone tells me they are new to *The Cloud* and asks me which edition they should read first, I always point them to Acevedo Butcher's.

Imagine my delight when I heard of Acevedo Butcher's latest project—a translation of Brother Lawrence's *Practice of the Presence*.[2] I reached out to her to express my interest, and eagerly agreed when her editor asked me to read the manuscript prior to publication, in the hopes that I might offer some words of praise that they could use for marketing purposes. When the manuscript arrived, I set aside all my other reading and dove in. As I expected, the words of Brother Lawrence came alive in a vibrant and inviting way, thanks to Acevedo Butcher's facility with language and skill as a translator. Again, she had taken a centuries-old classic of mystical literature and made it vivid, exciting, and relevant for our times.

But reading Acevedo Butcher's version of *Practice of the Presence* also surprised me in an unexpected way. In her introduction to the book, she comments on the vexing problem of gender in language, and how it's not always easy to convey the sometimes subtle gendered meanings of a text when it is rendered in a new tongue. Add to that the even more challenging question of how gendered pronouns unavoidably say something about our image and view of God, and that such pronouns often can carry subtly

---

1. Carmen Acevedo Butcher, *The Cloud of Unknowing with the Book of Privy Counsel* (Boulder, CO: Shambhala, 2009).
2. Carmen Acevedo Butcher, *Practicing the Presence: A Revolutionary Translation* (Minneapolis: Broadleaf Books, 2022).

different connotations in different languages. All this leads to a translator having to make significant choices when deciding how best to convey an ancient author's words—including pronouns and other gendered words—in a meaningful contemporary way.

Acevedo Butcher describes Brother Lawrence's own deeply Trinitarian spiritual as "binary-surpassing," and she goes to say, "The representation of God in this translation has a home in pronouns 'they/themself/theirs.' These signify the trinitarian mystery of Love, the friar's leitmotif, and limn the image of the Trinity's community, or perichoresis."[3] In other words, she felt that Brother Lawrence's own inclusive spirituality made it reasonable to render his voice, in English, speaking of God using the so-called "singular they"—pronouns such as *they*, *them*, and *theirs*, preferred by many people today who want their pronouns to transcend and/or include both of the "binary" genders (male and female).

The singular they pronouns are associated in our day with transgender and nonbinary persons. But to apply these pronouns to God? It made sense to me. In fact, I wondered why I hadn't seen this done before. In all honesty, I'll admit I stumbled a few times over sentences like this (italics added): "Since you are aware that God is present before you during your actions, that *they* are in the deep center of your soul, why not stop your activities and even your vocal prayers, at least from time to time, to love God, praise *them*, ask for *their* help, offer *them* your heart, and thank *them*?"[4] Even though the point behind the "singular they" is to read these inclusive pronouns as applying to an individual and not to a group, it can still be an adjustment for an old-timer like me. Like most people in the Abrahamic traditions, I am hard-wired to see God as *one*—I even stumble over the "royal we" in the biblical creation story, "Let us make humankind in our image, according to our likeness"

---

3. Acevedo Butcher, *Practicing the Presence*, 35.
4. Acevedo Butcher, *Practicing the Presence*, 48.

(Genesis 1:26 NRSV). Acevedo Butcher's translation of Brother Lawrence reminded me that even those of us who are strong allies of the transgender/nonbinary community can sometimes struggle over the singular they (and other inclusive pronouns).

Acevedo Butcher stated that she applied the singular they to Brother Lawrence's voice because "these pronouns also respect the good kind news inherent in the gospel: *All are welcome.* When I read these words, I can breathe. And I hope they do the same for others, opening space for every person and for Mystery."[5] I applaud her, and support her doing so—and I believe any awkwardness someone might feel when discovering the singular they is a small price to pay for stretching our language to be more inclusive and just. But I realized, in reading this text from a contemplative perspective, that God's pronouns can invite us into the heart of the mystery of gender—not only in relation to God, but in terms of our human identity as well.

Let us begin with God. Like so many people of my generation, I grew up in a suburban Christian church where God was presented simply using masculine language: Father Almighty, Lord God, King of Kings, and so forth. But we have a long tradition in Christian history of recognizing that to apply a single gender to God like that is limiting. The fourteenth-century English mystic Julian of Norwich became celebrated in our time because of her visionary proclamation: "As truly as God is our Father, just as truly is God our Mother."[6] Today, I suspect most people would say the remarkable thing about that statement is the fact that Julian, immersed in the relentlessly patriarchal medieval church, could see and articulate this universal truth even six hundred years ago. I believe we can equate Julian's insight with Galatians 3:28 (NRSV): "There is no longer Jew or Greek, there is no longer slave or free, there is no longer male

---

5. Acevedo Butcher, *Practicing the Presence*, 35–36.
6. Julian of Norwich: *The Showings*, trans. Mirabai Starr (Newburyport, MA: Hampton Roads Publishing, 2013), 163, Kindle Edition.

and female; for all of you are one in Christ Jesus." Saint Paul seems to be saying that membership in the body of Christ renders mundane categorizations like our ethnicity, political or economic status, or even gender, ultimately far less important than the life-giving love of God, which transcends such earthly categories.

Paul, of course, is talking about our human experience. But remember Genesis proclaims that we human beings are created in the image and likeness of God. An exclusively patriarchal, masculine image of God is unacceptable because it automatically excludes half of the human family. If we replace the exclusively male God with an exclusively female Goddess, that's just turning the problem inside out rather than solving it. Meanwhile, if we say that God is genderless, that runs the risk of making God so abstract as to render God irrelevant or unrelatable to *everyone*. So we are left with a mystery: a God who both transcends *and includes* our human gender spectrum: fully human, fully masculine, fully feminine—and even more than that.

If God is more than just a "father" (or, for that matter, a "mother"), then how do we relate to God, using the familiar categories of human gender? I've heard people speak of the "Mother-Father God." Others choose to avoid gendered language altogether, preferring to speak of the "Creator" and "Savior" rather than the "Father" and the "Son." As we struggle to make theological and spiritual sense that God is more than just a boy or a girl, our language will unavoidably have its awkward and clunky moments. We can bristle at such seeming lapses of literary elegance, but I think a more skillful response would be to welcome even cumbersome attempts to find new ways to speak to—and about—the God who is greater than our earthly gender binary.

This leads to a question that some might find scandalous, and others might find smacking of heresy, but that I believe is one of the sacred questions of our time: Is God nonbinary? If that is a new word for you, here's a definition from the website of the Gay and Lesbian Alliance Against Defamation (GLAAD):

> Nonbinary is a word used by people who experience their gender identity and/or gender expression as falling outside the binary gender categories of "man" and "woman." Many nonbinary people also call themselves transgender and consider themselves part of the transgender community. Others do not. Nonbinary is an umbrella term that encompasses many different ways to understand one's gender.[7]

Gender is a profound mystery, and so much of the language we traditionally use to describe gender can be criticized as stereotypical or limiting. Men are strong, aggressive, competitive, athletic, and proud, while women are compassionate, gentle, sensual, cooperative, and nurturing. Even as I write these words (merely for the purpose of illustration), I wince at how they seem to pigeonhole both genders. If someone truly embodies the gifts of masculinity *and* femininity, does it make sense to say their gender identity or expression exists beyond the binary? So often our understanding of God emerges out of our understanding of ourselves. For me, seeing God's gender as nonbinary makes perfect sense, because it tracks with my own experience.

I still remember the first time I met someone who identified themself as nonbinary. It was at a neighborhood program in my local community for artists-as-activists, where one of the speakers introduced themself using that term. Being unfamiliar with the word but also being a writer, naturally I looked it up. I discovered that nonbinary is related to a cluster of words, mostly neologisms, that have emerged since the 1980s and 1990s to describe gender diversity and gender variance, especially beyond the binary of male and female. Words like genderfluid, gender-expansive, genderqueer,

---

7. In Focus: Nonbinary People, GLAAD Media Reference Guide, accessed October 12, 2022, https://www.glaad.org/reference/nonbinary.

gender-nonconforming, and demigender all convey slightly different and nuanced ways of gender identity and expression. Neither
male nor female, indeed! But also profoundly meaningful for me.

I was born in 1960, which means my childhood and adoles-
cence stretched from the final days of the Eisenhower administra-
tion to the murder of John Lennon, the week I turned twenty. I was
assigned male at birth, although back then no one talked about it
like that. Just "It's a boy!" But as my childhood unfolded, my boy-
ness seemed to be a bit off-kilter. In fact, I came to think I was
something of a failure as a boy. In my family and neighborhood,
markers of masculinity included sports, hunting, fishing, working
on cars, and developing physical strength—yet I remained stub-
bornly uninterested in all these things. Granted, on occasion I tried
to "be a man," but only for the sake of fitting in; after a couple of
seasons of going hunting with my dad, I felt so relieved when I
finally found the courage to tell him I really didn't like it and
wouldn't go with him anymore, even though that meant a loss of
time we spent together. My interests skewed more toward the arts,
toward poetry and music and painting. And I also was interested in
fashion, although I could barely admit that even to myself. And let's
just say it wasn't just boys' and men's fashion that caught my eye.

As it turned out, I was not the only one who could see that
my gender didn't quite line up with the cultural expectations of
our time. Other kids would point out to me (or tease me) for
running, laughing, acting like a girl. Friends, trying to be helpful,
would counsel me to try to tone down my femme mannerisms and
body language. And kids who weren't interested in being my friend
would bully me, an easy target since I was such a "girl."

I don't recall ever feeling any sort of all-pervasive gender dys-
phoria, at least not in the way that transgender persons like Nicole
Maines or Jazz Jennings have described it: an "insistent, persistent,
and consistent" sense of being a girl in a boy's body (or vice versa).
When I heard about famous transpersons like Christine Jorgenson

or Renée Richards, I thought they were interesting, but I never had the sense of "that's me." I had no sense of being in the *wrong* body altogether, just a kind of awareness that I wasn't entirely at home with the expectations placed on me for being a boy—but I knew that I would be just as much a misfit if I had been born with a female body. There was plenty that I liked about being male, even with all my natural girlishness. Grasping for language to make sense of myself, by the time I was an adult I would say "I'm very androgynous" or "I'm really in touch with my feminine side." Carl Jung's ideas that everyone contains both a feminine *anima* and a masculine *animus*, and that one of the goals of maturity is to integrate both dimensions into our individuated psyche, resonated deeply with me.

I lived more than a half century before I stumbled across concepts like nonbinary or genderfluid. I suppose if I were born a generation or two later, I might have known—and embraced—those concepts for myself, even at a young age. And I especially wonder if, in my childhood I had been exposed to an image of God that encompassed the entire gender spectrum (with nonbinary pronouns to match), I might have been spared plenty of angst as I tried to make sense of who, in fact, God created me to be.

As I write these words, I see that they represent a coming out, and I suppose some people might find them startling or even shocking. But to me, it's no big deal—or at least, I don't think it ought to be a big deal. Once I understood that nonbinary gender identity is a thing, I said to myself, "Oh, so *that's* what folks like me are called."

So why make a fuss over God's pronouns? Why embrace a nonbinary image of God?

I say this shouldn't be a big deal, but I also understand that for many people, struggling to know and accept their unique, beautiful expression of gender—especially when it emerges beyond the binary—is a matter of profound importance. It is embarrassing, but honest, for me to admit that I spent much of my life concealing my own gender expansiveness simply because I have the privileged ability to do so. Since I am biologically masculine, for the most part express my gender as male, and am happily married to a wonderful cisgender female, I could easily leave my own gender identity safely locked away in the obscurity of my private life. In all candor, the introvert in me would gladly do just that. But I write these words at a time when transgender persons—including nonbinary persons—have become the target of more and more political scapegoating. Some people oppose trans girls and women participating in girls' and women's sports, arguing that their assigned-male-at-birth bodies give them an unfair advantage. Public restrooms have become another flashpoint for controversy, thanks to the baseless claim that predators might pretend to be transgender persons in order to invade bathrooms and victimize others—even though in fact transgender persons are the ones most likely to *be* victimized by transphobic assault. Some states are even creating barriers for transgender children and even adults to receive gender-affirming care.

Scapegoating is one of the most insidious and shameful ways in which human beings hurt each other. Jews, Muslims, Blacks, Asians, Pacific Islanders, indigenous persons, poor people, disabled persons, immigrants, refugees, lesbian, gay, and bisexual persons, and transgender persons, are just some of the groups that get targeted, whether by hostile individuals or by unscrupulous politicians who manipulate the fears of their constituents for their own gain. If we take Jesus seriously, with his consistent message of love and compassion and reconciliation with all people—a message my late friend and Trappist monk Brother Elias Marechal calls "radical equality and inclusivity"—then we realize that scapegoating is wrong—no matter which groups or persons are targeted.

Each of us needs to look within and consider what we can do to dismantle scapegoating, both within our own hearts and within society at large. One way we can do this is by acknowledging our solidarity with persons and groups who are the target of scapegoating—even if we have access to privileged ways of avoiding such targeting ourselves. For example, as an educated white person who presents as male, I have access to resources and safe spaces that provide me with greater personal safety and protection than is available to many others who do not have the same privileges I do. But if I am willing to acknowledge my own "difference"—in my case, being genderfluid—then I have taken an important first step toward allying myself, like Christ, with those who have been hurt by the injustices of our broken world. Of course, we can be allies with those who are hurt by our system even if we do not identify with them (and perhaps for contemplatives, one of our tasks is to identify ourselves with all who have been marginalized, excluded, or traumatized by the "lousy, rotten system"[8] that shapes our world).

But if the question of God's pronouns points to the mystery of gender and the problem of gender-related injustice in our world, how does the contemplative life equip us to respond to issues like these? I can only answer this question on a personal level, but I hope my experience might be helpful for others. My journey as a practitioner of contemplative spirituality has equipped me to meet the mystery of God and gender in several ways.

My own experience of being outside the gender binary certainly contributed to challenges I faced both as a child and an adult, including the occurrence of anxiety and depression. Mental health challenges are, unfortunately, a common issue for nonbinary, genderfluid, and transgender persons. I was fortunate in that I had access to therapy, which became an important resource for learning to foster my own mental health and wellness. But as an important adjunct to therapy, I discovered that developing a stable silent

---

8. "Lousy, rotten system" (often misquoted as "filthy, rotten system") is from an interview with Dorothy Day that was published in the February 18, 1970, issue of *National Catholic Reporter*—https://www.ncronline.org/news/people/dorothy-days-filthy-rotten-system -likely-wasnt-hers-all.

prayer practice significantly aided me to gently and kindly accept myself just as I am—thereby also helping to alleviate the suffering that depression and anxiety caused.

Contemplation also proved to be an essential means for deconstructing toxic images of God that I received in childhood. I've already noted how the God of my childhood, very much a "guy"— an old white man in the sky, complete with Gandalf-esque beard, but he (yes, "he") was angry, judgmental, difficult to please, and easily provoked to fury at the slightest hint of disobedience—or nonconformity. And while learning healthier theology was an essential step on my journey of healing my toxic image of God, just as important was the experiential practice of learning to be vulnerable before God in stillness and silence. It wasn't easy, given the scary God that I had to overcome. But as I became more and more comfortable in my own body and began to see that the God I met in silence was a God of love rather than wrath, I slowly began to trust the God of my experience more than the God who was a projection of other people's fear.

Finally, contemplation also created a spaciousness within myself that made it possible to truly encounter people who were different from myself, and/or different from mainstream ideas that I had internalized, with a sense of openness, wonder, curiosity, and acceptance. A confession: I can be as judgmental and biased as the next person, especially toward people who I perceive as "other." But an ongoing contemplative practice, for me, has been a way for me to unclench that part of my psyche that reacts with immediate judgment to new people and situations. It has been said that mysticism is the antidote to fundamentalism; I think we can expand that to say that contemplation is an antidote to scapegoating. Jesus taught his disciples to refrain from judging others—and while I do believe that thoughtful *discernment* is both psychologically and spiritually healthy, I see the mandate to suspend judgment as an invitation to meet people where they are, to listen to their stories, and to respond with compassion and care, rather than fear, aggression, or exclusion.

So the practice of contemplative forms of prayer has helped me to love myself better, to love God better, and to love my neighbors better. This has been a long process. As I've noted, for many years I saw my femme qualities as embarrassing or even shameful—evidence that I was just a failure as a male. That narrative did nothing for me other than to contribute to my experience of shame, depression, and anxiety. Contemplation, however, has helped me to simply accept myself as I am: no big deal. Since contemplative spirituality has helped me to find God's unconditional love, in agreement with the wise words of Julian of Norwich, or Carmen Acevedo Butcher, such spirituality has helped me to recognize God as far more expansive, inclusive, and affirming than I had been led to believe. Finally, a sustained practice of contemplation has fostered in me an increasing experience of being loved and being capable of love—both of which translate into being more available to meet people where they are and to respond to those who suffer or have been oppressed in whatever helpful ways I can.

Since "in Christ there is neither male nor female," does it follow that God includes both (or all) genders? Is this a heresy for our time, or a radical way to know God more truly and deeply? Thanks in part to Acevedo Butcher's affirming use of the singular they/them/their as God's pronouns, I am increasingly persuaded that it is deeply true to say God is nonbinary. I for one am comfortable with this idea, seeing it as no more radical or outrageous than our historical idea that "God is male" or the equal-but-opposite "God is female." Practically speaking, I suppose most people will continue to project on to God whatever gender expression they find comfortable, and I'm okay with that too—as long as we don't let our ideas about God and gender turn into an excuse for excluding or scapegoating others. But maybe the ultimate gift of meeting God in silence is not having to make some final determination about God's image or gender or anything else about God. Rather, we meet the One who simply loves us, in caring and compassionate silence. In that silent, still, present moment, anything is possible (Matthew 19:26)—including the vision of a world where all genders and gender variations are loved, cherished, and accepted.

I try to be a committed ally to the LGBTQ+ community, and yet even with my own nonbinary identity, I did struggle, especially at first, with Acevedo Butcher's use of the singular they to describe God. So I try to be compassionately understanding that many people (especially folks my age and older) might find it difficult to embrace the expansive but unfamiliar image of a nonbinary God. But I hope anyone who is committed to creating a world shaped by community and reconciliation (rather than privilege and scapegoating) will graciously undergo the awkwardness of learning to embrace the singular they as a pronoun for trans and nonbinary persons—and for God too! God's pronouns can help guide us to creating a better world where all genders are welcomed and affirmed.

I began this essay by talking about how much I admire the work of a good translator. Let me end with one more thought about the mystery of gender. The more I think of it, the more I believe that gender seems to be its own type of "translation." Gender exists as a way for us to translate the experience of love into our embodied lives. To be embodied is to be a person who is gendered; some of us do this in masculine ways, others in feminine ways, and still others in expansive or fluid or nonbinary ways. Perhaps embodied gender is as much a part of the way we mortal beings express love as dialects and accents are an essential part of how we express language. People who speak different dialects or with different accents may sometimes have difficulty understanding one another, but with care and attention and a mutual effort at understanding, such linguistic barriers can be overcome.

Doesn't gender work the same way, only in terms of how we express and experience love? After all, gender is such a central part of our experience of being human: it impacts not only our romantic and sexual lives, but our friendships, our ways of relating to family and neighbors, and even how we select our interests, passions, and personality traits. We joke about how men and women seem to come from different planets, and I suppose genderfluid and non-binary folks therefore must come from yet some other celestial bodies. But like varieties of dialects, our many expressions of gender reveal how richly diverse we are, but do not have to function as firewalls between us. There can be tremendous joy and fun in discovering how different we are from one another, even though we also need to know all the ways we share common ground.

If we take nonbinary identity seriously, we can see that gender is a mysteriously beautiful spectrum rather than a rigid, dualistic dichotomy. We are all invited to learn what it means to be human in the context of our many different ways of expressing gender. As long as it is love we're working with, it's all good. We may have many different types and expressions of gender, but they all point to one love: the love of God. That love is available to us in many ways, through romance, friendship, kinship, but also through the encounter with God that comes to us through contemplation. May we learn to receive the embodied love of others, love that is refracted into our lives through the shimmering beauty of the mystery of gender—even when expressed in creative, unusual, or out-of-the-mainstream ways—with wonder and acceptance and joy.

2

Listening for the Holy

Sarah Forti

e can listen to respond, we can listen to understand, or we can listen with the intent to love. All three of these intentions can overlap, but the intention to love must be supported by other foundational beliefs and spiritual practices. This type of holy listening can be directed toward God, our neighbor, and the self to bring about healing and reconciliation in our bodies, our communities, and our world.

I thought that I was a good listener, being a quiet and introverted person, but it was not until I lost my hearing that I started learning to listen for the holy. I was not born with hearing loss; hearing was something that I lost slowly during my twenties. It happened so gradually that I had plenty of time to be in denial. I started to compensate for the loss without realizing it, leaning in closely during conversations or watching people's mouths to identify the shape of words. I watched for body language and facial cues regarding when I was expected to respond or answer a question. I did not want to admit that I had a problem, and I did not identify as a person with a disability. I was desperately trying to stay in control of something that I did not know could be taken away. I was trying to anchor myself in a previous and passing reality with no compassion for my condition. The irony is that I was a church music director, and I could not hear my own choir.

I have worn hearing aids for over a decade now, and I can acknowledge that losing my hearing only magnified an inner deafness that I did not know was there. Even when I did hear, I was not listening for the holy. I fell into a cycle of listening to respond and responding to receive approval.

Lately, it has felt like I've been moving toward a precipice, and this feeling brought to mind a vision that I had twenty years ago. I was walking on a high plateau toward the edge of a cliff. Jesus was walking next to me, but he was not slowing down as he approached the edge. He was going over. He was going beyond. Right before he stepped off the edge, he extended his hand toward me. I felt as if he were inviting me to go with him, but that he would not stop his work to wait for me. He was not staying there, and it was my choice whether or not to go with him. Without hesitation, I took his hand and we stepped off the edge. Jesus flew, and I held onto his hand as we traveled high above a pine forest.

This vision came back to my mind as I recalled the return of the feeling of moving toward the edge. For years now, I have felt called to grow in my love of my neighbor. I have felt called to listen for the Holy in those who differ from me in ability, race, gender, orientation, or politics. For years now, I have also avoided many of those topics that so often trigger hostility, criticism, and debates (which to me feels like jumping off a cliff). What I realized is that I have been grounding myself in the affirmation and approval of those around me, as if their uplifted hands were the plateau that I walked on. What if pursuing risky conversations, such as reconciliation and inclusion, is like jumping off a cliff of perceived social support?

I have learned that contemplative practices often involve a pattern of relinquishment and letting go. This does not only include what we grasp with our hands, but it could also mean letting go of our perceived grounding. Holy listening forfeits anxiety over trying to fix, change, manage, or control the situation that we're in. I can name within myself that I have a deep fear of rejection and conflict, and this informs my listening habits. I am tempted to fall into patterns of subtly managing conversations to maintain the false grounding of their support. These tendencies come from a desire to control conversations in order to feel safe, but I have come to understand that we are not listening for the Holy in conversations that we are trying to control.

Holy listening is a commitment to be fully present, releasing the other person from our assumptions, judgments, and prejudices to receive more freely what is being offered. What has helped me to relinquish control is to find my true grounding, to remind myself every day that God's presence and God's love are the ground of my life and identity. This helps me put my faith in a wider, more generous reality than the list of worst-case scenarios that I am tempted to anticipate.

I have learned to practice holy listening with God through prayerful silence. Understanding this helps me to relinquish control and not to attempt to achieve or accomplish anything other than simply being present with God. I am inspired by Lady Julian of Norwich who, in her fourteenth-century vision of God's love and Christ's passion, heard the Lord say, "I am the ground of thy praying—first, it is my will that thou have something, and next I make thee to want it, and afterwards I cause thee to pray for it."[1]

An Invitation to Prayerful Silence

Take a moment to remember the fullness of the presence of God as the ground of our praying. Receive God's presence as a precious gift, with nothing but your own full presence to give in return.

> O Lord, you have searched me and known me. You know when I sit down and when I rise up; you discern my thoughts

---

1. Julian of Norwich, *Revelations of Divine Love*, trans. Fr. John-Julian (Brewster, MA: Paraclete Press, 2015), 93.

from far away. You search out my path and my lying down, and are acquainted with all my ways. Even before a word is on my tongue, O Lord, you know it completely. You hem me in, behind and before, and lay your hand upon me. Such knowledge is too wonderful for me; it is so high that I cannot attain it. Where can I go from your spirit? Or where can I flee from your presence?[2]

Through my Shalem mentor, I learned the importance of prayerful body compassion. This practice invites holy listening within oneself and one's body, acknowledging without judgment our condition and our needs in the sight of God. This is also a powerful reminder for those of us who are managing illness, injury, stress, or trauma to be compassionate witnesses to our own stories.

An Invitation to Body Compassion

What in my body is most in need of my loving attention? Take time to become aware of the presence of the Holy, whose love is active and attentive. Remember that you are God's beloved and receive God's love as if it were given graciously and directly into your area of need. What in me is most in need of God's loving attention?

> Blessed be the God and Father of our Lord Jesus Christ, the Father of mercies and the God of all comfort, who comforts us in all our affliction, so that we may be able to comfort those who are in any affliction with the comfort with which we ourselves are comforted by God.[3]

If we are not given patterns and rituals for how to give love and grace to ourselves, then we may not know how to give love and grace to others. This body compassion moves beyond body consciousness

2. Psalm 139:1–7 (NRSV)
3. 2 Corinthians 1:3–4 (ESV)

toward the belief that God is fully present and fully loving "at the lowest part of our need," as Julian of Norwich said, for "God does not despise what he has made."[4]

Even before losing my hearing, so much of my identity was upheld by trying to meet expectations, gain and maintain approval, and avoid rejection at all costs. I was deaf to the voice of God calling me the beloved, and how that same voice calls the person I'm in conversation with the beloved as well. Acknowledging and receiving God's love directly into the context of our wounds, struggles, and anxieties can then ground our authentic selves in that love, overcoming our inner deafness and receiving the voice of God calling us the beloved. Through grounding ourselves in a spiritual identity as God's beloved, we can offer that love both to ourselves and to others through holy listening.

From our center of being grounded in contemplative practices, we can choose to listen for the Holy by receiving the other as a whole person, not merely their words, but God's intention for them as his beloved. This is supported by God's invitation to ground ourselves in a merciful and expansive landscape beyond our fears and defenses. We all may be broken now and offer sharp shards to one another in conversation, but spiritual grounding in God's compassion for ourselves and our brokenness can help us to welcome others with hope, seeing God's desire for their healing and wholeness. This is a gift of relinquishment that we can give to one another, seeing God's presence and God's love as a wide and generous grounding that extends to the other person so that we entrust them to that love. Julian reminds us, "He looks upon us in love and wishes to make us partners in His goodwill and deed, and therefore He moves us to pray for that which it delights him to do."[5]

---

4. Julian of Norwich, *Revelations*, 17.
5. Julian of Norwich, *Revelations*, 100.

An Invitation to Contemplative Intercession

Name a specific request for prayer that you would make to God and imagine that you are holding that desire in your right hand. After naming that intention as your own, hold your other hand open to hear and receive God's intentions, which may be illuminated through prayerful silence and our relinquishment of control.

> Trust in the LORD with all your heart,
>   and do not rely on your own insight.
> In all your ways acknowledge him,
>   and he will make straight your paths.[6]

In this posture of holy listening, I am fully present to you as you are now, but I also celebrate and receive God's intentions for you as you will be, forgiven, healed, and whole.

Listening for the Holy can happen in conversations, it can happen in prayer, and it can happen within our bodies. In any of those places, it still involves relinquishment of control and a willingness to trust the grounding of God's love more than we trust the ground that we walk on. In my life, listening for the Holy is supported by small practices: practicing silence, practicing relinquishment, practicing being centered and grounded in love. This helps us to create space to listen for what is being invited, rather than operating from a grounding of assumptions about what is needed or necessary. This inner displacement of assumptions while listening can also help us to pause the temptation to analyze the person under a prayerful magnifying glass.

In his theological novel *Lilith*, published in 1895, George MacDonald says, "To understand is not more wonderful than to love."[7] I am still tempted to listen to respond; however, it has become even more tempting to listen for understanding. If the desire to

---

6. Proverbs 3:5–6 (NRSV)
7. George MacDonald, *Lilith* (St. Petersburg, FL: Compass Circle, 2020), 57.

understand does not also lead to a desire to love, then it is still just another way that I am measuring my worth, ability, and proficiency. I can spend so much time analyzing another person's words (and my reception of those words) that I am not led to love. Listening in order to love does not abandon the desire to know and be known; it deepens and enriches the pursuit of understanding. When we pursue understanding through the eyes of love, then we are opening ourselves to receive wisdom from holy listening. Listening with the intent to love does not abandon the desire to respond, rather it sets us free to respond from a place of God's abundance rather than from the scarcity of our perspective. Julian describes this abundance as planting ourselves in fertile soil, saying, "Our Lord is the ground on which our prayer grows."[8] How would our relationships be different if we began our listening not only with the desire to understand and respond, but with the intent to love?

In *Lilith*, there is a scene where there is an entire host of walking skeletons representing those who only after perishing were able to find their humanity. MacDonald describes their skeletal forms, which have eyes but do not yet have faces.

> Did they know how they each appeared to the others—death with living eyes? Had they used their faces, not for communication, not to utter thought and feeling, not to share existence with their neighbors, but to appear what they wished to appear, and conceal what they were? And having made their faces masks, were they deprived of those masks, condemned to go without faces until they repented. . . . They will by and by develop faces, for every grain of truthfulness adds a fiber to the show of their humanity.[9]

This description of the skeletons being deprived of the masks they fashioned in life speaks to the truth of the fear and control

8. Julian of Norwich, *Revelations*, 152.
9. MacDonald, *Lilith*, 48, 53.

that must be stripped away when listening for the Holy. The mask that we wear to maintain the false grounding of social control stops us from truly seeing ourselves and others as the beloved, and it is a mask that we need to remove again and again. Relinquishing our perceived power to be made vulnerable is a subversive and courageous act of love for one another, and it is just one example of *kenosis*, or self-emptying, which Jesus modeled through his entire life of teaching, healing, and self-sacrifice.

In his commentary on Julian of Norwich's *Revelations of Divine Love*, Denys Turner describes this vulnerability as being the true face of love. He writes, "It is perhaps Julian's central theological insight that sin wages war against love because sin is of its own nature violent, but love wages no wars at all, not even against sin, for love is absolute vulnerability. Love knows no other strategy than that vulnerability."[10] This is where we are led when listening for the Holy. We are led to the desire to love. We are led to a vulnerability that reveals our true face, our neighbor's true face, and God's true face, the face of love. In our relationships and conversations, what are the obstacles to listening for the Holy? What are the obstacles to listening with the intention to love? What are the obstacles to vulnerability, and meeting true-face to true-face with God and neighbor? How can we bring holy listening into conversations with people who differ from us in ability, appearance, national origin, race, orientation, politics, and faith?

Holy listening is an act of surrender to the Holy Listener in our midst, trusting that God listens with the intent to love and to reveal God's true face. In this practice, God is the ground of our praying, God is the source of reconciliation, and God is the movement that empowers us to grow into the latter while rooted in the former. Like a seed that must go into the ground and die to itself

---

10. Denys Turner, *Julian of Norwich, Theologian* (New Haven, CT: Yale University Press, 2013), 21.

before growing forth toward transformation, we are invited to let go of what we think is needed to receive what is being invited. The ground of holy listening is a space that can break open the seed of the heart: "The sacrifice acceptable to God is a broken spirit; a broken and contrite heart, O God, you will not despise."[11]

May the Holy Listener who calls you "beloved" unbind you from the graveclothes of fear and self-preservation. May the Holy Listener, who is the ground of your praying, be for you the fertile soil for the dying of masks and the rising of true faces. May the Holy Listener, who is present at the lowest part of your need, lead you home to the intention of love; "for perfect hope is achieved on the brink of despair, when instead of falling over the edge, we find ourselves walking on air."[12]

---

11. Psalm 51:17 (NRSV)
12. Thomas Merton, *No Man Is an Island* (Boston, MA: Mariner Books, 2021), 218.

3

Contemplative Collegiality

Caring for the Souls
of Black Biblical Scholars

Gay L. Byron

"We bear witness not just with our intellectual work but with our-selves, our lives."

—bell hooks

As the #BlackLivesMatter movement was rising to a heated pitch during spring 2020, I was teaching my New Testament courses online as a result of the COVID-19 pandemic. I was also pastoring a church due to an unexpected turnover in leadership. Using the same desk for the virtual delivery of lectures and sermons challenged me to remove a wall or the well-constructed boundaries that had marked my identity as a biblical scholar. This unintentional intersection of my professorial responsibilities with my priestly commitments has caused me to ask questions about the meaning of my scholarship, the purpose of my teaching, and the scope of my vocation. I have already reflected on such matters,[1] but now much more is at stake. In the face of the unrelenting swath of murders stemming from police violence

---

1. Gay L. Byron, "My Society of Biblical Literature Journey: Service, Scholarship, and Staying Connected to the Call," in *Women and the SBL*, ed. Nicole L. Tilford (Atlanta: Society of Biblical Literature Press, 2019), 157–166.

and other forms of white supremacist terrorism, as well as the sudden and ongoing loss of lives from a virus that at that time was raging without an end in sight, I began to lean ever more deeply on what Howard Thurman calls "disciplines of the spirit." I now realize that the very spiritual practices that have sustained me in my personal and professional life have not been publicly disclosed in my scholarship. It was not until 2020–2021, when I was in a clergy residency program sponsored by the Shalem Institute for Spiritual Formation[2] that I finally had a context to enable me to put words around the necessity of circles of collegiality, communities of accountability, and models of support and care. Through this program I experienced "contemplative collegiality," a phrase I coined to capture what happens when colleagues dare to be vulnerable with one another and find ways to work through cultural differences, microaggressions, and other forms of subtle racism that creep into our classrooms and other spaces of teaching, learning, and worship.

What Is Contemplative Collegiality?

At the same time that I was connecting with a new set of clergy colleagues in the Shalem program, my Society of Biblical Literature (SBL) colleagues were hosting a virtual Symposium on #BlackLivesMatter.[3] These colleagues whom I have admired over the years shared stories of how they negotiated unfamiliar and often unwelcoming spaces in academia. They offered reflections on the lessons learned, the struggles encountered, the paths pursued to find more healthy ground, and the questions that still linger in the face of institutional roadblocks and other forms of

---

2. "Going Deeper: Clergy Spiritual Life and Leadership," Shalem, August 13, 2020–July 12, 2021, https://shalem.org/programs/going-deeper-clergy-spiritual-life-and-leadership/.

3. "#BlackScholarsMatter: Visions and Struggles; Lessons and Hopes," SBL, August 12–13, 2020, https://www.sbl-site.org/meetings/blackscholarsmatter.aspx.

systemic racism that keep them consumed with "invisible labor." This invisible labor (primarily evidenced by an inordinate amount of committee work as a representative or spokesperson of one's ethnic group, or in some cases all People of Color) leads to fatigue, burnout, and poor health outcomes.[4] This may account for why, as of 2019, women of African descent in the SBL account for only 3.4 percent of its approximately 8,000 members.[5] During the Symposium, my colleagues noted the importance of mentoring and the value of finding space and opportunities to share their stories and unique ways of interpreting biblical texts. They also discussed the isolation, loneliness, and lack of collegial support that sometimes hindered their progress and even caused them to walk away from the traditional path of academic advancement measured by the tenure clock.

The Shalem program on Clergy Spiritual Life and Leadership gave me space and time to step away from the academic metrics that defined my understanding of accomplishment and offered a framework and a community through which I could become more intentional about self-care, Sabbath-keeping, and contemplative-mindfulness. To put it more precisely, I entered the experience pondering, *Why are my spiritual and self-care practices cut off from my scholarly life?* These new clergy colleagues offered a safe space for tearing down the internal wall that was blocking my full productivity as a biblical scholar *and* a religious leader. There were eighteen participants in the program, and I was assigned to a smaller cohort of six who would meet during the first summer intensive residency and continue meeting monthly until the second summer intensive. We called ourselves the "Coast to Coast" group, with participants in every time zone, from California, Wyoming, Iowa,

---

4. Mary-Frances Winters, *Black Fatigue: How Racism Erodes the Mind, Body, and Spirit* (Oakland, CA: Berrett-Koehler Publishers, 2020), 109–35.

5. Society of Biblical Literature, 2019 SBL Membership Data Collection, retrieved March 3, 2023, https://www.sbl-site.org/assets/pdfs/sblMemberProfile2019.pdf.

Pennsylvania, Washington, DC, and Florida. We bonded instantly around a shared desire to deepen our respective ministries through cultivating spiritual practices such as silent retreats, deep listening, and caring support of one another across miles and through virtual meetings. We never met face-to-face during the entire program, but our care for one another was palpable. In addition to this peer support, I formed a listening group of laity from my congregation for another level of spiritual deepening and mutual support and accountability. In this regard, I invited my congregation as a whole, and this laity circle in particular, into my process of learning a new way of serving in leadership in our faith community. The outcome of all this connectivity was an ethos of personal and congregational care, trust, and discernment based on deep listening. This is contemplative collegiality.

What Does Contemplative Collegiality Look Like?

In theory, contemplative collegiality involves accountability, engagement, connection, mutual support, and deep listening—all for the purpose of creating spaciousness where there is mutual belonging, indwelling, and opportunities for discernment. But what happens when our best intentions do not materialize? When disconnections happen and old patterns and ways of doing things take over when expedient decisions need to be made? What happens when institutional structures don't match the realities of individuals called to lead or contribute to the goals of the group or organization? What happens when we realize there is still so much to learn about the ways in which we have been formed by our experiences and misinformed about the experiences of others? This is when it is useful to have another angle for reflection, another approach for decision-making, another perspective through which to respond to awkward, difficult situations with grace and compassion. This is when colleagues who have been on the journey, who have taken the bumps, who have traveled the detours, and even pulled over on the side of the road to rest and regroup can offer the gifts of presence, encouragement, and accountability.

As wonderful as the first residency of the Shalem program was in offering spiritual resources, guest lectureships, and overall spaciousness for nurturing the spirit and connecting with like-minded peers, there was an overall awareness among the Black participants in the program that we were being immersed in a contemplative experience that was still overwhelmingly Eurocentric in orientation and leadership.[6] In addition, there was an incident at the end of the program during which one of the leaders unwittingly shared a piece of music that harkens back to a stark image of slavery—a whipping post.[7] After a colleague brought this to his attention, our leader offered an apology to the group via e-mail on the following day, but there was no acknowledgment of the incident in the group's final plenary session. His well-intentioned message to the group fell into the abyss of silence. We finished the session with expressions of gratitude despite the "unfinished business" that lingered in the air. The Black sub-cohort of participants met and discussed the incident and, as is often the case, reached out to the director and leader to express our concerns and to ask for more education and awareness around cultural metaphors and racialized imagery that on the surface is innocuous, but can be hurtful and polarizing to those who are still reckoning with the trauma of slavery and other injustices.

---

6. Shalem has since that time addressed this imbalance in its readings and programs. In 2021, Shalem held a gathering of Contemplatives of Color (Black, Indigenous, and People of Color [BIPOC]) who had participated in its programs since its inception back in the 1970s. The first gathering was held virtually on September 25, 2021, for the purpose of sharing experiences and devising strategies and resources for expanding program offerings.

7. "Whipping Post," song by The Allman Brothers Band. Accessed May 18, 2022. https://www.google.com/search?q=whipping+post+lyrics.

In retrospect, I was inspired by my colleague's willingness to acknowledge his lack of sensitivity and his unintentional offense, and even more encouraged by the fact that I could engage him around this microaggression and know that regardless of this misstep, we have a common thread of trust that enables us to speak candidly and to learn from each other without judgment, impunity, or fear. Indeed, the teachable moment was missed when the incident occurred during the first residency, but the leadership took time to reflect on the incident and responded to the feedback from the Black cohort by taking ownership of the work *they* needed to do. One specific action resulted in a seminar during the second residency on "Learning from Stumbling," designed to provide a guided opportunity for all the participants to reflect and share any concerns or learnings related to the incident. This was facilitated by an African American woman, a former Shalem program participant and current Board member.

Throughout this session, I found myself disconnected from the discussion because it seemed "too late"—a whole year had elapsed!—but this gave the non-Black participants in the group an opportunity to reflect more deeply on the incident, and also to get a glimpse of the "invisible work" the Black participants had been doing all along, well after we had returned to our primary ministry responsibilities. This session also created space for deep listening and personal and communal accountability. The facilitator slowed things down and created space for reflection and discernment on how best to move forward. Indeed, apologies were registered. Yet, the real work and the true learning from this "stumble" will be evidenced in the sustainable practices and policies the leaders of the organization will put in place so that a safe and hospitable environment is created for every participant in the program. In other words, "a contemplative organization [is] an organization whose structures and processes mirror its mission . . . an organization that walks its contemplative talk."[8] Likewise, each facilitator and pre-senter, in particular those who are still carrying the invisible knap-sack of white privilege, are being called to take on the responsibility of learning more about the history and culture of BIPOC (Black, Indigenous, and People of Color) communities.[9]

Caring for the Souls of Black Biblical Scholars

So what does all of this have to do with Black biblical scholars? The notion of contemplative collegiality that has come into sharp focus for me over the past couple of years has taken place in a con-text of care: first and foremost, self-care, imbued with spiritual practices; secondly, community care, informed by deep listening; and thirdly, caring for the souls of those in my realm of influence. While pastoring, this involves my parishioners. As a professor, this involves my students as well as faculty and staff colleagues. And as a Black biblical scholar, this involves a recognition, with deep grat-itude, of those who have come before and paved the "stony road," and a commitment, with deep hope, to those who are coming after to carry on the legacy of African American biblical scholarship.

Divinity schools, seminaries, universities, and professional guilds are beginning to write policy statements and implement DEI initiatives to address what can no longer be hidden behind surface efforts of inclusivity. In addition, books about racism, antiracism, whiteness, white privilege, and the like have been written and con-tinue to multiply in a market-driven publishing world that now sees the *value* of Black lives. The work of Black biblical scholars

---

8. Margaret Benefiel and Bo Karen Lee, eds., *The Soul of Higher Education: Contem-plative Pedagogy, Research, and Institutional Life for the Twenty-First Century* (Charlotte: Information Age Publishing, 2019), 132.

9. Peggy McIntosh, "White Privilege: Unpacking the Invisible Knapsack," *Peace and Freedom*, a publication of the Women's International League for Peace and Freedom, July/August 1989, retrieved April 28, 2023, pp. 10-12. https://psychology.umbc.edu/wp-content/uploads/sites/57/2016/10/White-Privilege_McIntosh-1989.pdf.

is not simply the work of scholarly production, though now more than ever monographs, edited volumes, peer-reviewed articles, critical essays, public discourses, podcasts, and other platforms for the dissemination of our scholarship are endless. But until *we* start to do the necessary work of caring for our bodies, caring for our souls, and caring for one another, those who hold the reins on institutional infrastructures will continue with business as usual. I suggest contemplative collegiality is one way of doing this care work. As the late bell hooks has so poignantly observed, "We bear witness not just with our intellectual work but with ourselves, our lives."[10] If we say that Black Lives Matter, then it will take more of us to model how to put this into practice.

The virtual desk that housed my Bible for sermons, the textbooks for my classes, the sick-and-shut-in list of my parishioners, and the contact information for my colleagues is the place where I realized the value of my spiritual practices and the need for contemplative collegiality. The Shalem Institute gave me an opportunity to experience collegiality in a new way through care, trust, and discernment. This essay has focused on care work for Black biblical scholars and all those who have a stake in teaching the next generation and transforming the SBL into a place for "fostering biblical scholarship" that recognizes the multidimensional lives of Black biblical scholars.[11]

This essay first appeared as "Contemplative Collegiality: Caring for the Souls of Black Biblical Scholars," in Black Scholars Matter: Visions and Hopes in Africana Biblical Studies, *ed. Gay L. Byron and Hugh R. Page Jr. Used by permission of SBL Press.*

10. bell hooks, "Embracing Freedom: Spirituality and Liberation," in *The Heart of Learning: Spirituality in Education*, edited by Steven Glazer (New York: Penguin Group, 1999), 122.

11. Gay L. Byron, "Contemplative Collegiality: Caring for the Souls of Black Biblical Scholars," in *Black Scholars Matter: Visions, Struggles, and Hopes in Africana Biblical Studies*, ed. Gay L. Byron and Hugh R. Page Jr. (Atlanta: SBL Press, 2022), 145–51.

4

From Censorship to Contemplation

Silence in Queer Life

J. M. Smith

When I first came out as gay, I was both nervous and excited. It was exhilarating to see a previously unspoken barrier break down that had separated me from others for so long. A great relief came over me whenever I shared more of myself with those who I perceived as supportive friends, family, and community.

At the same time that I began coming out to my community in my early twenties, I became more and more enamored with the practice of contemplative silence. Initially, I think this gravitation toward silence felt like an escape from the pressures and negotiations of myself and my surroundings. I felt a great pressure within me to maintain a sense of personal safety in the context of a highly divided world, both in the church and public life, on the status of LGBTQ persons. I was learning how to negotiate between self-disclosure and censoring myself in varying degrees depending on how much the space appeared welcoming to queer lives or not.

But, over time, I realized that the truth of contemplative silence and living out a queer life were much more complementary than I first thought. For they both, in their own way, exposed who I am, and that the nature of reality is more mysterious and more loving than I initially grasped. Contemplative silence allowed me to reclaim silence as a practice of dwelling more deeply in divine reality rather than simply a powerful means of control and censorship wrought with pain and diminishment of self. Contemplative silence affirmed that my life is grounded in more than what I can know or control. Queer life has helped me understand that we are indeed more obscure, more unknowable, than we may think, and each day is an offering to love ourselves and others as our lives unfold day to day.

"Out of the Depths I Cry . . ." (Psalm 130:1, NIV)

Initially, before coming out, I felt anxious and uncomfortable both with myself and with others. The social stigma around being anything but straight became isolating and silencing for me. Contemplative and mystic John O'Donohue in his text *Eternal Echoes* explores the human soul's restlessness and inherent desire for belonging, and the various conditions that keep human beings from feeling a sense of true connection to themselves and others.

Donahue lists the gay community as one that struggles deeply with belonging due to a fear of social stigma. He invites his reader to spend time living in the mindset of someone afraid to speak out about their sexuality: "Imagine the years of silent torment so many gay people have endured, unable to tell their secret."[1] The "silent torment" that Donohue describes is a state that resonates for me. My silence caused me to close in on myself; I became cautious to share more generally for fear that the "secret" of my sexuality would somehow be consciously or unconsciously found out by others. I

---

1. O'Donohue, 113. John O"Donohue, *Eternal Echoes: Celtic Reflections on Our Yearning to Belong*, Reprint (New York: HarperCollins Publishers, 1999; repr., New York: Cliff Street Books/Harper Perennial, 2000). Citations refer to the First Cliff Street Books/ Harper Perennial edition.

found myself silencing myself out of a sense of social stigma and internalized shame.

What's more, even after breaking out of the silence, this wrestling around coming out can be a long and never-ending tussle. Or more often, for me, a subtle negotiation. I discovered after the initial thrill of finally coming out that I had started an ongoing process, rather than performed a grand finale. To this day, I am perpetually aware of how much I disclose about myself and my identity to others.

O'Donohue goes on to name the fear that compounds the silent torment of staying silent: "Then, when they declare they are gay, the hostility that rises to assail them."[2] This hostility, while perhaps not a predetermined reality, is often something that I still find lurking as a possibility in the back of my mind.

Before engaging with a community, I try to feel out the space. Is it dominated by normative gender roles implicitly or explicitly? Does the space communicate an explicit welcome to LGBTQ persons? Or is it just unclear either way? I often decide how to present myself, what to say or what to censor from my story, depending on my assessment of my surroundings.

The church is no exception to my cautious scrutiny about its welcoming nature. Whether evangelical, Protestant, or Catholic, Christian community has been in conflict about the status of LGBTQ persons for decades. At times, people of faith insist on the inclusion of LGBTQ persons as equally beloved by God. Exclusionists argue, among other things, that queer persons are a deviation from God's original intention for human beings, and therefore not condoned by the Church. What is little appreciated is how the very arguments themselves can be hard to endure as one listens to others debate the status of your life and loving relationships.

In social and political life, LGBTQ lives continue to be threatened and explicitly silenced. The recent state bans on books that

---

2. O'Donohue, *Eternal Echoes*, 113.

express queer life that are occurring in Oklahoma, Florida, Texas, and other states are an explicit censoring of LGBTQ life. In Florida, the "Don't Say Gay" bill prohibits teachers from discussing sexual orientation or gender identity to children kindergarten through third grade.[3] The transgender community has been especially hit hard. The suicide rate among trans persons—particularly among teens—remains high.[4] Recently, in Indiana, the 5th Circuit court upheld the right of a Catholic hospital system to deny gender-affirming care to transgender persons.[5]

In light of these cultural and political contestations over queer life, LGBTQ persons can live with a great deal of shame about their sexuality and gender identity. Shame is, as John O'Donohue remarks, "a powerful emotion . . . that penetrates to the core of the soul." He names that shame imposed by social condemnation is inherently inhospitable: "There is no graciousness or light in the language of shame. It is a language spoken without compassion or respect."[6] Without a sense of welcome, one can quickly become devoid of true connection with others and one's self.

This shame is only compounded by the practice of self-censorship. The silence of censorship constricts the soul and makes one feel small. This is a silence that demands discipline of the mind. It stifles the life of the full person and restricts one from connecting to oneself and others. It is exhausting.

---

3. For more on this topic, see Elizabeth A. Harris and Alexandra Alter, "Book Ban Efforts Spread Across the U.S.," *New York Times*, January 8, 2022, https://www.nytimes.com/2022/01/30/books/book-ban-us-schools.html. Also, Jaclyn Diaz, "Florida's Governor Signs Controversial Law Opponents Dubbed 'Don't Say Gay,'" *National Public Radio*, March 28, 2022, https://www.npr.org/2022/03/28/1089221657/dont-say-gay-florida-desantis.

4. "Facts about LGBTQ Youth Suicide," The Trevor Project, December 15, 2021, https://www.thetrevorproject.org/resources/article/facts-about-lgbtq-youth-suicide.

5. Bobby Nichols, "Appeals Court Rules Catholic Healthcare System May Deny Care to Transgender Patients," New Ways Ministry, October 10, 2022, https://www.newwaysministry.org/2022/10/10/appeals-court-rules-catholic-healthcare-system-may-deny-care-to-transgender-patients/.

6. O'Donohue, *Eternal Echoes*, 113.

The LGBTQ community has fought back against this censorship in a variety of ways. For one, the word "queer" has (controversially) been reclaimed by some in the LGBTQ community. Previously, generations saw it as having a purely derogatory connotation. Additionally, in the 1970s, the Pride movement began crying out on the streets of New York City: "We're here. We're queer. Get used to it!" The bright colors of the rainbow flag, born out of the same movement, stand as a sign around the world for LGBTQ pride and a celebration of love.

"Close the Door, and Pray . . ." (Matthew 6:6, NIV)

At the same time that I was expressing myself more fully in the world, intentional silent prayer became a safe haven for me—even in some ways an escape or a respite from the stresses of navigating a heteronormative world. I sought out practitioners; I began to visit a small closet-like devotional space in the basement of the seminary's larger chapel building to practice centering prayer. I remember an altar and icons displayed at one end, and an old church pew situated against the right wall. Sometimes, when I was sitting to pray, I would hear the laughter and chatter coming from above me in the building's common space. It was a place to quiet my being.

The silence of contemplative prayer felt familiar—ironically because I had been practicing silence about my sexuality for many years. Against the abundance of critical voices within and without, the practice of silent prayer was one thing I could do without judgment, or at least far less judgment than other aspects of my life. Repeating a word over and over felt like permission to let my mind be like my fingers fiddling with a piece of string or like my hand moving back and forth through a container of sand.

"O Lord, You Have Searched Me and Known Me" (Psalm 139:1, NKJV)

Over time, my practice of contemplative silence began to involve much more of myself than I could have initially anticipated. While at first, the prayer practice was a kind of relief or escape from my constant vigilance and self-consciousness, over time, once it was no longer novel, I found that the prayer practice was less and less able to bring me the same relief. I became bored, restless, and even more anxious and judgmental of myself for being bored and restless!

As solitary contemplative Maggie Ross warns in her discussion of silence, many remain in a sort of "elementary meditation" because they are "more interested in justifying who they are or fantasizing who they might be."[7] This was certainly true for me at first. I wanted to sit quietly and pray in order to watch myself being good or being prayerful. It was a way of validating my sense of self beyond external pressures.

For many of us, the practice of contemplative techniques can simply be an extension of what we do in the rest of our life. As Ross remarks, we want to watch ourselves and construct a sense of self through our own preconceptions, images, and thoughts. We might sit silently only to convince ourselves that we are diligent and good at sitting still. We may seek to create a sense of self that is more peaceful, more loving, or we may seek to gain control over our mind.

While these are not bad things to desire, Ross is suggesting that contemplation is more than this. Contemplation is expectant waiting for That Which Is. Our relationship to That Which Is cannot be solely accessed on the level of what Ross calls "self-conscious mind," but rather what she names as "deep mind." Self-conscious mind is that part of ourselves that is self-regarding;

---

7. Maggie Ross, *Silence: A User's Guide*, vol. 1. (Eugene, OR: Cascade Books 2014), 33.

it holds our perceptions, images, and concepts. The deep mind constitutes what others may understand as the spiritual heart or the unitive dimension of reality. It is direct, immediate, and "holistic."[8] Self-conscious mind meets the deep mind at the blurred dimension of liminality, in Ross's schema. Ross emphasizes that it is—by very definition—distinct from our self-consciousness. Contemplation in her schema is waiting for, as Ross says, "whatever irrupts—often unawares—from the deep mind."[9]

Contemplation involves a willingness to let our preconceived notions, our programs, and our own sense of control to fall away. It may even mean, Ross provocatively writes, "to let 'spirituality' fall away in unknowing."[10] Too often even our sense of "spirituality" can get in the way of releasing and resting in deep mind. Ross is quick to say that this "unknowing" does not mean that we are no longer conscious or that our mind stops working. It is, rather, that our "awareness of linear rationality of self-consciousness" ceases.[11]

To know something means that it has been categorized by our mind into an object to be known, and is then given a name or subject in language in order to communicate to others what we know. But words by their very nature separate and categorize; they create an object and a subject. Linguists debate language's meaning, wondering if a word is truly referential to something in the world, or simply given meaning only through its difference from other words. In whatever way we understand language, it is constructed and referential, and therefore creates distance between one thing and another, between ourselves and others.

While language and knowing separate and distinguish life, the contemplative stream trusts that all that is, all that exists, is ultimately unitive. Language is not identical to what exists, and

---

8. Ross, *Silence*, 14.
9. Ross, *Silence*, 47.
10. Ross, *Silence*, 34.
11. Ross, *Silence*, 48.

therefore existence can be properly referred to as unknown and without distinction. What's more, we might acknowledge that we ourselves in our own existence participate in this deep reality of that which is without distinction. The process of contemplative silence keeps us perpetually aware that our truth is not rooted in prescribed language but rather speaks back that our existence is always more than any linguistic reference can say.

So, to approach the immediacy of the present moment or the fullness of That Which Is, we must trust that we ourselves participate in this reality, and then practice contemplation as a way of actively acknowledging something more than that of which we are conscious. As Ross writes, this does not mean that the mind ceases to operate, but rather there is a suspension of self-consciousness, in order to allow the "deep mind" to do its work.[12]

For Ross, the truth of ourselves involves the deep mind, and is not simply something that referential language can contain nor our conscious self-regard ever fully know. Ross writes:

> The everyday self-conscious mind has a small capacity. It tends to get caught in feedback loops of its own making. It is full of preconceptions, fixed ideas, and images. It is where the imaginary construct we think of as "self" resides, as differentiated to the unfolding truth of the self that inhabits the silence of deep mind. This unfolding truth of the self is a combination of the decisions and responses we have made in life and openness (or not) to be trans-figured in deep mind by its shared nature with God.[13]

This idea of the person's "unique unfolding truth" Ross names connotes a dance between our everyday self-consciousness and our "deep mind."[14] We must forget ourselves for a time in order to come to ourselves and to the holy.

---

12. Ross, *Silence*, 49.
13. Ross, *Silence*, 42.
14. Ross, *Silence*, 42.

For me, to practice silence as more than an escape hatch out of the many pressures and fears of my life meant that I had to radically trust a reality greater than myself. Trusting something other than myself is a radical ask when one's very sense of self feels constantly threatened by the world.

As someone who has lived with a profound sense of self-consciousness, the practice of something else, of ceasing control, is daunting and risky for me. To move from this sense of self-consciousness to contemplation means to relinquish the very sense of self that is defined by my own self-conception—even and including by the language of sexuality and gender altogether.

Over the years, since I first began to come out, I have found that the articulation of who I am is an ongoing process, always negotiated as I move through the world and always discovered upon further reflection. Each morning, I find myself waking up and having to ask myself again, "Who am I today? How will I express myself? What will I share and not share about who I am to others?"

And this is where the reality of queer life and the reality of contemplative silence coincide for me. For the truth is, my life has been more than even the terms of sexuality and gender have given me. How I relate to the world and my relationships over the years have always looked unique in such a way that any language of identity, while necessary, feels just a bit inadequate.

Identity work, like contemplative prayer, can ultimately bring us to a similar conclusion, that we are indeed always a bit obscure to ourselves. There are aspects of ourselves—those dimensions of our being that are aware of a deeper mysterious reality—that are inaccessible to language.

After listing about ten different common arguments for LGBTQ inclusion in both the church and in theological understandings of God, queer theologian Linn Marie Tonstad writes, "Most fundamentally, many of these [queer] arguments ignore the ambiguities of human existence, the ways in which our lives and their consequences are neither transparent to us nor fully within our power to determine."[15]

Later in the discussion, Tonstad outlines how theorists have argued that binary gender norms are not stable and therefore are not, contrary to what some argue, natural. Secondly, since these binary conceptions of gender are not in fact a given, certain traits associated with men and women are not in fact essential to any particular gender. Identifying these positions is certainly critical. But Tonstad notes that while these arguments are important, they are not actually going to become the silver bullet to overcome oppressions. This is because as creatures, we are not as self-determining as we may think. Tonstad confesses that, indeed, "we *aren't* self-transparent, rational, autonomous individuals."[16] She writes:

> Recognizing that heteronormativity, patriarchy, and racism shape both ourselves and the world we live in is certainly important. The diagnostic tools of critical thought help us to see that they so shape us and how they do so—both in the sense of what about us they shape, and in the sense of the strategies they depend on. Awareness of the world's deformation by what many theologians call the powers and principalities—powerful, destructive forces that nonetheless shape us at deep levels, and from which we long to be freed—is akin to a conversion or mystical experience. Subsequently, one sees the world and one's own experience through new eyes. Or, perhaps one has always known about these deforming powers because one has always been targeted by them.[17]

To push against these practices, as she says, "remains a lifelong project that starts anew each day. It's never complete or finished."[18]

---

15. Linn Marie Tonstad, *Queer Theology: Beyond Apologetics* (Eugene, OR: Cascade Books, 2018), 47.

16. Tonstad, *Queer Theology*, 71.

17. Tonstad, *Queer Theology*, 71.

18. Tonstad, *Queer Theology*, 71–72.

For both Tonstad as a queer theologian and Ross as a mystic, the human being is never fully known to oneself and is perpetually living out the "unfolding truth" of one's life. The queer life and the contemplative life, then, are not so far apart in their premise: at root, the life of the human being is much more obscure, profound, and mysterious than we sometimes give away. We are each day rising to meet that mystery—both the aspects that we try to describe or at least mark with words, and the rest that is forever emerging and is more than what language's referential devices can fathom. The process of contemplative silence keeps us perpetually aware that our truth is not rooted in prescribed language but rather speaks back that our existence is always more than any linguistic reference can say.

Each time I sit down for quiet, each time I sit in contemplative silence, it is a different moment. My self-conscious awareness is always relating to what it cannot know, but in a different moment from the one previous. Likewise, each time I articulate or express my love of others and myself, it is never finished, never final, yet offered.

While still risky, my queer identity is something I see as a gift, for it has given me a way of living that is more loving, more spacious, and more trusting of That Which Is. It led me to embrace the obscurity of the human life. Moving from the silence of censorship to the silence of contemplation helped me to understand that my life is inextricably connected to the great reality in which all of life breathes and moves. For this and much more, I am thankful.

5

Toward a Decolonising Spiritual Direction Practice

Weeping, Gnashing Teeth, and Opening to the [Ancient] New

Althea Banda-Hansmann

n the Western Cape Province, South Africa, where I reside, Black, indigenous, or persons of colour (BIPOC) spiritual directors desperately need a place where we are free to be our full selves and can experience the full spectrum of our lived experience in places of deep rest as we train as spiritual directors. My hope is that we would not be burdened or retraumatised consciously and unconsciously by white Western curriculums of spiritual direction practice, as is the current reality of spiritual direction teaching. My hope and desire is for a new generation of South African and global spiritual direction teachers who are committed to modelling integrated contextual consciousness and anti-oppressive and trauma-reducing approaches in the design and delivery of spiritual direction training. This is an especially important modality for participants from historically oppressed groups and particularly for Black[1] people in South Africa.

---

1. In South Africa, Black people is a generic term for people of colour who are citizens of South Africa by birth or descent or naturalised before 1994. Black means Black Africans, Coloureds, Indians, and includes Chinese naturalised before 1994.

From what I have heard and read in selected assigned articles, the quality of contextually conscious, spiritual direction education deteriorated after 1993 when the Shalem Institute of Spiritual Formation partnered with the then Institute for Christian Spirituality, now known as the Centre for Christian Spirituality, to deliver spiritual direction training in the Western Cape. This was the first and only time Shalem Institute conducted this training here. Back then, it would seem that the curriculum integrated the development of social consciousness and an understanding of racial identity formation under Apartheid as a core part of spiritual direction training. I completed my spiritual direction training between 2018 and 2020, and the curriculum was devoid of an understanding of the South African context, the history that the Dutch Reformed Church and most White churches played in sanctioning Apartheid, the Black Church's struggle against Apartheid, and trauma and the transformation of trauma from a spiritual direction perspective.

My Story toward a Deeper Seeing

On 7 June 2018, I sat in a circle toward the end of day two of the first module of a two-year spiritual direction programme in the predominantly white-owned farm land of Stellenbosch, South Africa. I was one of five Black participants in a class of twenty-five participants, of whom twenty were white. I had already been present in class with cognitive dissonance from an earlier session in the day when a white guest theological teacher from the faculty of Theology at the University of Stellenbosch taught us about our "spiritual heritage." In teaching us about our spiritual heritage in South Africa, the teacher did not include any BIPOC spiritual leaders and/or contemplatives from Sub-Saharan Africa. As this teacher left, I walked fast to reach her before she left. I asked the teacher where the teaching about our Black struggle for social justice and spiritual heritage was. I mentioned Steven Biko, Desmond

Tutu, Beyers Naude, the Church struggle against Apartheid, and so many other Black and white spiritual leaders of South Africa, and why they were not represented. She acknowledged the absence of this spiritual heritage and replied that it all still had to be written up. While many South African Black contemplatives and spiritual leaders in the fight against apartheid produced written words and published works, and while many freely available online videos exist of our Black spiritual leaders, what the teacher meant was that these perspectives still needed to be written up by educators like herself.

In the last session, toward the end of day two, I asked the programme's four white spiritual direction teachers if we would be learning about spiritualities that speak to our South African experience of colonisation, the trauma of Apartheid and oppression. One of the teachers responded and said, "No, we are not. If you want to look at trauma, you could do Trauma Release (TRE) work, outside of the spiritual direction programme."

I was astounded at this response that, in 2018, delinked contextual consciousness from the spiritual direction curriculum design, teaching methodology, and practice—a response that failed to create an inclusive environment for all South Africans. My mind, body, and soul were in profound grief, disappointment, anger, and dissonance with the lack of contextualised spiritual direction training for a South African current reality. The teachers' paradigm reflected a spiritual direction training programme designed by a team of white-only facilitators who had not considered and developed a curriculum centred in awareness and responsiveness to South African conditions, a responsiveness to the damage of Apartheid, to Black lives and a sense of self, or to other historically oppressed groups and the damage done to white lives and sense of self. The training programme was centred on white spiritual norms and values, and perpetuated the development of an individualistic spirituality. The teachers and the programme design avoided systemic issues that impact South African communities, institutions, families, individuals, and relationship dynamics. They failed to acknowledge and teach about the lived experience of oppression, the presence of God amid oppression, and the opportunity for healing that is present in what people say or don't say when they share their stories in spiritual direction sessions.

Our South African society suffers from the effects of political, historical, and vicarious racial, abandonment, enmeshment, and personal trauma, gender-based violence, physical abuse during childhood, and criminal violence. The implications are psychological, physical, mental, spiritual, familial, communal, institutional, and systemic; trauma impacts the resilience of our social fabric and the hope of future generations. A contextually conscious, anti-oppressive, and trauma-reducing approach to spiritual direction holds seeds of awareness and wisdom about how God can be at work in spiritual dimensions of trauma and our healing. It links individual suffering to the broader psychosocial conditions in which most people live, and brings awareness to colonial and Apartheid dynamics found in the experience and language of trauma.

I was the only Black person in the class that openly voiced pushback about the lack of contextualised curriculum. I am not aware of any private challenge given by any of the other participants to teachers about the white-centric approach to spiritual direction training in the Western Cape Province. It seemed, given my challenge, that the teachers responded by assigning these two books: *Theology Brewed in an African Pot* by Agbonkhianmeghe E. Orobator,[2] and *Joy Unspeakable: Contemplative Practices of the Black Church* by Barbara Holmes,[3] as well as the article "Evolving Approaches to Spiritual Direction in South Africa" by Annemarie Paulin-Campbell

---

2. Agbonkhianmeghe E. Orobator, *Theology Brewed in an African Pot* (Maryknoll, NY: Orbis Books, 2008).

3. Barbara Ann Holmes, *Joy Unspeakable: Contemplative Practices of the Black Church*, 2nd ed. (Minneapolis: Fortress Press, 2017).

and Puleng Matsaneng[4] as additional recommended individual reading. While the curriculum centred Ignatian Spirituality, none of the teaching faculty taught the class from the works of Orobator, Holmes, Paulin-Campbell, or Matsaneng, or from any other tenets of African spirituality or the spirituality that arose from the struggle against Apartheid. All the aforementioned would have been relevant to what we, as potential spiritual directors, might encounter as we accompany directees from oppressed or marginalised populations. This reality that I encountered also points to the development needed on the part of spiritual direction teachers to witness the movement of God in others and to hold space for all aspects of life with God in South Africa and in other similar or different contexts of oppression.

It is my observation that in the Western Cape, spiritual direction training is led by white middle-class Christians, who rarely practice an understanding of how systems of power impact the spiritual formation of historically oppressed groups and white Christians. This stands in stark contrast to the demographics of South Africa, where 92.2 percent of the population is Black and 7.7 percent of the population is white.[5] My first two days of spiritual direction training were a painful further awakening to the dire need for a spiritual direction curriculum and practice that speaks to the lived experience of most people in our country. Our teachers in the programme were experienced in offering spiritual direction and education in primarily white, middle-class South African contexts, and this orientation permeated the overall teaching, programme design, learning environment, materials, and assessment elements, learner experience, and which voices and views were centralised or marginalised.

---

4. Annemarie Paulin-Campbell and Puleng Matsaneng, "Evolving Approaches to Spiritual Direction in South Africa," *The Way*, n.d., 16, https://www.theway.org.uk/back/523Matsaneng.pdf.

5. South African 2016 Census Population Stats by Race, Community Survey 2016, Statistical Release, Statistics South Africa, https://cs2016.statssa.gov.za/.

The following day, on 8 June 2018, I felt vulnerable as I courageously shared my heartbreak at the lack of integration of local South African realities of our faith struggle against Apartheid and the ongoing post-Apartheid transformation work that impacts spiritual direction practice. The recognition that God was with the oppressed and our faith leaders in that struggle and the impact of the struggle on our faith and spiritual formation was never acknowledged or taught. Furthermore, our experience of Apartheid and its related forms of oppression deeply affected both Black and white in our country and our experience of God.

I remember that I broke down and cried and questioned, "Am I cursed to be here, when I know another way?" Having led transformation and diversity, equity, and inclusion interventions for well over thirty years at industry levels, in corporations, educational institutions, nonprofits, and Christian organisations, I was astounded by the brazen lack of duty of care to train:

- spiritual directors with a contextual and socially conscious practice of spirituality;
- spiritual directors who would be able to practice responsibly and responsively in a country with high levels of violence, trauma, and a legacy of oppression; and
- spiritual directors who would know how to listen in an integrated way to the personal, relational, social, systemic, and collective experience present in the narrative of the directees in individual or group direction sessions.

Surely God's wisdom and presence is active in all of life, the personal, the interpersonal, the institutional, the collective, the systemic, the contextual, and in the cells and tissues of our bodies, and in our intergenerational realities.

In a later module, I asked the question, "What do we do, as spiritual directors, when we notice the systemic impact on the directee in the narrative of the directee?" I gave a hypothetical example of listening as a spiritual director of a person who might have been sexually harassed and harmed in the context of church life. The same teacher, who previously directed me to "trauma release work" outside of spiritual direction, replied that "spiritual direction is not concerned with the systemic, it is concerned only with the individual." For spiritual direction teachers within the programme, social justice, healing from racism, the systemic and the prophetic are delinked from spiritual direction practice, curriculum development, teaching, and assessment. The centrality of the individual is valued and delinked from a collective experience and the impact of oppression. Prioritising the individual's experience to the exclusion of developing a social and systemic lens is another hallmark of white Western understanding of spirituality and interpretation of God that is traumatising for historically oppressed groups.

There was something different that I knew in my bones, in my spirit, and in my relationship with God. This is why I had broken down in tears in the class and said out loud, "Am I cursed to be here when I know of a different way?" The same teacher that I referenced earlier encouraged me to stay. I stayed because I felt a call to practice spiritual direction.

Toward the end of the two-year spiritual direction training programme, I decided to take eight additional months of extended self-study outside the formal curriculum to read, research, and have conversations with spiritual directors across the globe with a socially conscious, anti-oppression, and trauma-sensitive practice to produce a final paper that would help me think through a spiritual direction practice relevant for a South African context. The programme did not meet the needs of my Black self: seeking to be a spiritual director responsive to a people who hold so much of our collective experience of oppression and hopes in our bodies, our sense of self, our relationships, and our communities.

While a difficult and problematic spiritual direction training experience, I was grateful to see deeply into the state of spiritual direction training at least in the Western Cape. What I saw cannot be unseen or unexperienced. It inspires me to contribute to the field and practice of decolonising spiritual direction.

I am also grateful for the skills I acquired during the difficulty of my training. I appreciate learning to discern and ask questions in noticing the movement of consolation and desolation in a directee's narrative and life. I am grateful for two years of practicing the Examen prayer as a communal and personal contemplative prayer practice. I enjoyed reading two of the additional readings, namely *Sadhana: A Way to God* by Anthony de Mello[6] and *Theology Brewed in an African Pot* by Agbonkhianmeghe E. Orobator. While energy-consuming and not wishing the experience on any other BIPOC person under these circumstances, I appreciate my determination to take on an additional eight-month study before submitting my final paper to teach myself a way of spiritual direction practice that is both decolonising and empowering. This led me to deepen my existing network and build relationships globally with spiritual directors involved in different ways of decolonising spiritual direction practice. In this regard, I am grateful for conversations with spiritual directors at Shalem Institute for Spiritual Formation, Spiritual Directors International, and the Spiritual Directors of Colour Network, who nurture a relationship with me that includes the full reality of my lived experience. I appreciate the spiritual directors I networked with outside of the two-year programme who lived in the United States and South Africa, and the others I met through Shalem Institute—all helped me process and make sense of my experience of spiritual direction training. They encouraged my own and an overall spiritual direction practice that is contextually conscious, trauma-sensitive, and relevant for historically excluded and marginalised individuals and groups. Conversations and thinking with these spiritual directors on various aspects

---

6. Anthony de Mello, *Sadhana: A Way to God: Christian Exercises in Eastern Form.* (New York, NY: Image, 1984).

of decolonising spiritual direction practice and reading some of their written work have been encouraging and inspiring.

What Does Decolonising Spiritual Direction Mean?

The process of decolonising spiritual direction opens a deeper way of embodying spirituality and a wider perspective for listening to the presence of God in the lives of those we direct. It helps us to listen to the lifeforce in another way, along a spectrum from individual experience, relational experiences, institutional life, and the systemic. Decolonising spiritual direction invites us to release ourselves from the vestiges of colonial, Apartheid, and other oppressive habits that we inherited and that are still present in our individual and collective lives and in the practice of spiritual direction. Decolonising spiritual direction asks and invites us as spiritual directors to hold space for listening to multiple layers of trauma surfacing, coming up to be witnessed, held in light and love, and at times coming forth for continual release over time.

What Has Helped Me to Centre a Decolonising Spiritual Direction Practice?

At a personal level, decolonising spiritual direction is part of my practice in taking time to feel, notice, understand, and be in lifelong learning about the impact of oppression on my body and my nervous system. It is a choice to be increasingly aware of the effect of oppression on our collective body and collective nervous system. In my walk with God, decolonising spiritual direction is part of my learning to respond to God's call to rest, and in so doing release learned internalised and externalised habits of racial and other forms of oppressive harm. It means being in discerning community with others who support me and I them, in telling our truth while having the courage to sense, lean into, and/or imagine God's desire for us and for humanity. It means a practice of being in God's presence, opening to love and divine guidance in all spheres of life and welcoming the courage to create beyond white-centric approaches to spirituality and spiritual direction practice.

As a spiritual director, decolonising spiritual direction practice involves my ongoing commitment to be open to God's presence in me and to being skillful in how I hold space for directees to discern the wisdom in their bodies, give voice to the language of their nervous systems and memory, sense God, and reflect on the felt experience of their lived reality and social context. Decolonising spiritual direction practice is about listening to the individual or the group and noticing intrapersonal, interpersonal, institutional, and social systemic themes in their narratives. It is about entering and sensing God's love of another and of ourselves while facing life's struggles and joys. Decolonising our practice of spiritual directions invites us to heal from oppression by opening to a spirituality of witnessing others as they give voice to trauma, attending to what is calling for healing and the process of transformation.

The 4 Spheres of Healing from Oppression

The 4 Spheres of Healing from Oppression[7] framework illustrates two dimensions, relational and systemic, across four spheres of healing. These are areas to notice the movement of God's Spirit.

This framework describes the relational and systemic dimensions of decolonising spiritual direction practice in four areas. Work in any and all areas can be an outcome of or result in greater intimacy with God, healing, and opening to love. The work of decolonising at the relationship dimension grounds us in healing and renewal of self (intrapersonal healing) and our relationships with others (interpersonal healing). The work of decolonising at the systemic dimension

---

7. Althea Banda-Hansmann, 4 Spheres of Healing from Oppression for Spiritual Directors, Cape Town, Transforming Moments Consulting, 2020.

grounds us in healing and renewal in our organisations (the institutional body) and collective culture (the collective social body). These spheres of decolonising spiritual direction practice invite white and BIPOC directors to develop intimacy with God through and beyond our racialised identities and conditioning into superiority and inferiority. It supports us in acknowledging our BIPOC ancestors, their struggles and their gifts as part of our spiritual heritage, and as part of the foundation of spiritual direction training.[8]

The relationship and systemic dimensions of decolonising spiritual direction is a practice for our responsiveness and embodying God's image of us, in us. It is an active choice to practice healthier ways of being ourselves, being in relationship with one another, becoming healing leaders and institutions, and becoming healing societies fostering wellness and resisting oppression.

In closing, my hope is for a new generation of spiritual directors skilled in noticing God's active movement in the 4 Spheres of Healing from Oppression and embracing the imperative to decolonise in the twenty-first century. My desire is that a decolonising approach to spiritual direction will ultimately prevent those from historically oppressed groups who are seeking training as spiritual directors from further traumatisation, and that it will lead to relational and systemic healing. My dream is that a new paradigm for spiritual direction training realises the sacred wisdom and healing potential in BIOPC bodies. My hope is that healing will flow out to others, and that our communities, in the backdrop of trauma, will be changed over time, bathed in abundant love and life. I am thankful for the experience of my spiritual direction training, though it was painful and disappointing, because it allowed me to see clearly. God used the situation to impress even more on my heart, mind, body, and my vocation as a spiritual director the imperative of an integrated and decolonised spiritual direction

---

8. Alannah Earl Young and Denise Nadeau, "Decolonising the Body: Restoring Sacred Vitality," *Atlantis*, February 29, 2005, http://learnwhr.org/wp-content/uploads /I-Young-and-Nadeau-Decolonizing-the-Body-Restoring-Sacred-Vitality.pdf.

curriculum. We have work to do. In the words of Octavia Butler, this is succinctly narrated as: *"So be it. See to It."*[9] May it be so. Amen.

RELATIONAL-LEVEL	
HEALING SELF Healing internalised oppression. Healing trauma stored in the body. Inviting personal healing and contemplative practices for self-care, self-love and post-traumatic growth. Telling and rewriting our stories. Seeing and nurturing God's image of us. Deep rest in God and for the body. Developing the prophetic capacity and courage to be the uncomfortable voice for change.	**HEALING RELATIONSHIPS** Healing harmful, oppressive conditioned relationship patterns. Life-long commitment to unlearning superiority and inferiority-based behaviours. Inviting equality and difference. Developing compassion, understanding the world from one another's perspective. Cultivating relational empathy and care. Practising humility. Loving our neighbour.

OPENING TO LOVE

SYSTEMIC-LEVEL	
HEALING INSTITUTIONS Developing and showing up as healing spiritual directors and leaders. Life-long commitment to releasing conditioned patterns of superiority and inferiority. Producing socially conscious, equitable and trauma-reducing spiritual direction curriculums and teaching. Teaching how to resist injustice, rest in God and open to love. Creating supportive environments for decolonising, healing and transforming. Prioritising contemplative and traumareducing communal and organisational practices. Becoming healing and anti-oppressive spiritual directors and organisations.	**HEALING THE COLLECTIVE SOCIAL BODY** Healing multiple societal traumas. Welcoming collective decolonising practices now and into the 9th generation. Sustaining life-giving societal structures that generate healing and well-being in the collective body. Challenging unfair systems. Practising the spirit of Ubuntu. Generating communal contemplative practices. Honouring our ancestors, their struggle and gifts and ancestral territories. Remembering who we are, where we come from and who we are becoming in God.

© **Transforming Moments Consulting 2022, updated 2023**

---

9. "So Be It, See to It: From the Archives of Octavia Butler," *The Paris Review*, March 23, 2018, https://www.theparisreview.org/blog/2018/03/23/so-be-it-see-to-it -from-the-archives-of-octavia-butler/.

6

I Am

Joanne C. Youn

I am from China dolls hidden away on a shelf;
From out of reach mementos locked in curio cabinets.
I am from everywhere—100 countries over six continents,
and nowhere—for very long.
I am from soybean plantations whose stalks danced in the wind.
I am from textiles and trophies;
From Chen and Liu.
I am from pressure, performance, and from perfection;
From "only the best."
I am from Bible stories that were too often just stories.
I am from Hu Jing Hwua and Chen Er May;
From congee and potato chips;
From "unjust weights and corrupt scales;"
And from limited pies of affection and a poverty of love that stood
in contrast to material abundance and a child's collection of coins.
I am from these moments and more—too many for words,
when all I needed was less.[1]

Hobbled by the myth of the model minority, further exacerbated by our own cultural and familial contexts within the "American dream," Asian American identity has, perhaps more than any other American subculture, come to be defined in

---

1. Delivered on August 2, 2022, to the Abide Gathering in Big Sky, Montana, the inaugural conference of a new ministry with a mission to encourage Christian Asian Americans toward flourishing and deep relationships with God and others.

large part by its achievement orientation. To our great detriment, in an atmosphere where the goal is simply the next performance—whether personally, professionally, or in the church—there is very little room for authentic self-examination and relational flourishing.

I do not know many people who would rush to suffering, but for me it was the path to compassion, for myself and for others. When suffering is transformed by love into sacrifice, it becomes a holy and pleasing offering, true and proper worship.[2] In the past, I would have shied away from any suggestion that I had experienced hardship with enough magnitude or intensity to speak with any authority on the matter of either suffering or sacrifice. While this denial would have originated partly out of pride, it would have also—for the most part—been objectively true. I have worked on Wall Street, in Silicon Valley, in the major international financial center of Hong Kong, and in Washington, DC. There is no doubt that I have lived under the blessing of great abundance—both individually and communally. And yet, that abundance grew out of a cultural context deeply bound up in its stubborn denial of any need or insufficiency. Unsurprisingly, then, it was not until my late forties that circumstances led me to understand the intentional design, beauty, and strength behind the concept of interdependence. It is as much a testament to the Ivory Tower of my arrogance as it is to my achievements for me to confess that I sincerely believed I had never lacked for anything until that point in my life.

As my past identities proved themselves no longer sufficient to sustain me through the emerging circumstances of midlife, I committed to embracing self-awareness in order that I might experience God's presence in new ways. I longed to move forward in a brighter, more directed light, and to see myself through that light.

I am grateful to the Shalem Institute for offering the Heart Longings program, an online platform for spiritual formation

---

2. Romans 12:1 (NIV)

developed in the wake of the global COVID pandemic and in whose inaugural class I was honored to be a participant. At several different points during the Shalem program, I found myself desperate for God's comfort as I began to recognize some of my deepest-rooted false self-constructs, going all the way back to my early childhood. It was as though, just as a dark emptiness threatened to swallow me, a golden river of joy and freedom would come, as I once again discovered my true and ultimate orienting reality in its hues.

I recall a particular instance, at a large group session based on the work of Dr. Vincent Harding[3] entitled "Building the Beloved Community," during which the leader, very simply, asked us to share the name of our "mother's mother." I did not know at the time that this exercise would lead me to one of the most illuminating and yet profoundly painful journeys into my personal identity that I have ever undertaken. Sadly, as these parts of myself had never shown themselves to be of any commercial value or utility—in fact, quite the opposite—they remained unexplored and were nearly forgotten.

As it came time for me to share at the meeting, I stated that my mother's mother's name was not an American one. Looking back, this may have seemed like an obvious conclusion, and perhaps even been perceived as a throwaway comment, especially once I shared that she was not an American citizen, was born and raised in China, and did not even speak English until much later in life. What was surprising, however, is the fact that I found myself resenting the question itself, which sounded to me a bit too close to "But, where are you *really* from?" As I listened to everyone else introduce their grandmothers, in an effort to prove my own Americanness, I felt compelled to share the Anglicized name, "Eva," that she had been

---

3. Vincent Harding, preface to Howard Thurman, *Jesus and the Disinherited* (Boston: Beacon Press, 1996).

given when she obtained a Canadian passport sometime during my youth. I did so, even as I remembered that this was a name that my aunt had provided to her in jest, as my grandfather had once adopted the name "Adam" to make his Western business partners more comfortable while working together.

In the wake of a surge in violence against Asians and Asian Americans in this country and elsewhere around the world at the end of 2020, I witnessed the beginning of a collective awakening about what it is that we really wanted as individuals and as a community—what our hearts truly longed for, as well as the sobering realization that the ways in which we thought we would obtain those desires have, in fact, been woefully misguided. Reading about the struggles of the Black community in America showed me a two-fold reality: (1) I am a product and inheritor of a larger collective identity across history and time; and (2) it is not until I take responsibility for the choices that I make in light of that identity that I am able to fulfill the work that is mine to do in this world.

Physically and spiritually, I am part of a very specific family lineage. That story begins in China in 1865, when Hudson Taylor and sixteen other men and women established the very first China Inland Mission in my great-great grandmother's province outside of Shanghai. If not for their love of those who were clearly "other," it is unlikely that my family would have come to personally know the grace and mercy of God. Exactly one hundred years following those events, in 1965, my parents arrived from Taiwan to Los Angeles in the middle of the Watts race riots. After subsequently moving to New York in the hope of better employment, and wanting to do something about the injustices they saw in the systematic discrimination and economic inequality in this new land they had decided to make their home, they joined the congregation of Riverside Church in the Morningside Heights neighborhood of Manhattan. I did not realize until preparing for our group session that this was the church where Dr. King had spoken on a nearly annual basis in the eight years leading up to his assassination in 1968, or how close this church was to Central Harlem.

For too long, Asian Americans have bought into the lie that their success in America was tied to how "white" they could become. We were told that if we were just quiet enough or industrious enough, we would be accepted in this nation, built on the exploitation of both immigrants and enslaved people. As it was a common desire in many first-generation Asian families to ensure that their children would blend into their new environment without any hint of a foreign accent, even though it was her first language, my husband's mother refused to speak Korean with him after they arrived in the United States in 1971. This imposed an inherent limit on their ability to communicate with one another, which continues to this day. Unfortunately, his flawless English does not stop people from taking little-to-no care in the proper pronunciation of our four-letter last name. (Nor did it not stop their schools from requiring my children, who were born in the United States, to test out of English as a Second Language when they entered the public school system.)

My parents lived on a fraction of their earned income so that I could go to the most selective private schools and gain access to the most prestigious alumni networks for a future career where I could afford a house in one of the most affluent neighborhoods in the country. However, this did not stop multiple white women at the local high-end grocery stores on my street from yelling at me that I am the reason for all the bad things that have happened to America, nor did it stop local townies in Cambridge from yelling racial slurs at me across the street from Harvard Yard or the white men at the firm I joined after Yale Law School from believing that I could be treated like "Suzie Wong." Somehow, we are left perpetual sojourners, having left our homes for the promise of a better future in a place where we may never fully belong.

I often refer to an amazing quote from the July/August 2020 cover of *Yale Alumni Magazine*. In plain bold text, it proclaimed the sad truth, that "as a national community, we are engaging in the periodic ritual of being surprised by the deadly force of racism, when it has been with us all along."[4] For too long, Asian Americans stood on the sidelines, believing we would be insulated from harm and discrimination because, we were told, we were compliant "by nature." So, why then does Anti-Asian graffiti deface the halls of the nationally ranked high school that my sons attend, and why can they no longer bike the seven miles between our home and the US Capitol Building without legitimate fear of bodily harm?

Yet, as the psalmist declares, "Deep calls to deep in the roar of your waterfalls; all your waves and breakers have swept over me."[5] Chaos, as creativity in action, can be a useful agent of change. When efficiency, which implies that there is inherent value in the minimization of resource use, is conflated with effectiveness and becomes the framework for our choices, we subtly promote a world of finite resources in which altruism, or the giving up of our lives, makes no sense at all. We see sacrifice as wasted effort, and, with no room for mercy, remove from all our calculations those who would be considered "the least of these."[6] Yet, whereas hurry is the enemy of love, beauty is its extravagance. Life in the contemplative allowed me to confront the grief I carried, and to find in it God's invitation to grow in love, confront evil, and serve the excluded.[7]

My participation in the Shalem program coincided with a period of great shared repentance and humility and invited me to recognize what sustained righteousness actually requires. There is

4. Emily Greenwood, "Rewriting the End," *Yale Alumni Magazine*, July/August 2020, accessed February 27, 2023, https://yalealumnimagazine.org/articles/5180-rewriting-the-end.

5. Psalm 42:7 (NIV)

6. Matthew 25:40 (NIV)

7. Micah 6:8 (NIV)

so much we can learn from other minority cultures, and yet we were led to believe that there was only room at the top for one group and are continually pitted against diversity and affirmative action efforts fought on behalf of a better version of all of us.

It was at Shalem that I discovered how to be silent and, in the silence, an identity outside of what I did—specifically, what I did for a living—but instead based solely on who I already was. I was gifted with a new way to see myself and with which to orient myself toward God. In the quiet, I learned that my life is the granting of blessing from the Great "I AM" who tells me who I am.[8] I live in awe of the first stirrings of a new beginning and a new end. Just because something is difficult does not make it not worth doing. The breaking in our lives may be just as much for our strengthening, as for the strengthening of others. Even now as I discern a call in my life to remembrance and reconciliation, I marvel at God's invitation to be with Him and know that He is God, to be with Him, to simply be.[9]

---

8. Exodus 3:14 (NIV)
9. Psalm 46:10 (NIV)

7

Tell Me about Mary's Rage

Amanda Lindamood

Spirit of God

How does God touch their traumatized children, changing constantly
within a backdrop that demands they stay static?

How are those bodies tempted to surrender their truths for the possibility of belonging?

Their lips sing to the being that loves them from the deepest well,
your will be done, your will be done, your will be done.

The child's prayer becomes adult's tentative wisdom, passed from survived to surviving.

Do you know of a God that's . . . trusted?

Tender, loving joy more than your suffering?

This God is a presence, whose emphasis is not omniscience.

It's not an all-knowing universe that sustains hurting or healing; it's
truth that changes its meaning without telling lies.

It's the nourishing of wisdom, formed from childhood but believed
over lifetimes.

It's the believing that transcends community invitation to be well, now.

Now is quickly passing, quietly changing.

Ensuring we love what changes, especially what we need from a God
whose presence heals.[1]

began writing this essay the night I returned home from my
second time seeing *The Color Purple* performed at a local the-
ater near where I live. I had chosen this particular showing

---

1. Amanda Lindamood, "Spirit of God," 2022.

because it was followed by a moderated discussion with cast members. I wrote two poems that night that are woven into this essay and inspired by questions of God I am led to observe, though it wasn't until the third time I saw this performance that I could be in my body, present to a protagonist who is introduced as a fourteen-year-old mother and incest survivor. It is powerful to witness a poor, Black girl child sing her prayers to a baby that is about to be taken from her, and it brings a concreteness to God's perceived power and relevance. That relevance is personal, cultural, historical, and bodily, and it weaves experiences with needs and unmet needs, and community alienation and embrace. Intentionally, we are meant to feel this encounter and to see it repeating and evolving. God, our ideas of them, is becoming fluid instead of unchanged.

When I listen to Black, queer women and gender expansive cultural workers, I notice one repeating theme: valuing a cultivated ability to be present to their perceptions, to more than one thread of information at a time, and to experiences that challenge their beliefs. By some—like Audre Lorde in her poem "Contact Lenses"[2] and Alice Walker in her book *The Color Purple*—this is described as witnessing necessary truths about reality and about our own beliefs. In the words of Octavia Butler, this is succinctly narrated as: "God is change."[3]

Octavia Butler describes God in *Parable of the Sower*:

God is change—seed to tree, tree to forest, rain to river, river to sea, grubs to bees, bees to swarm. From one, many; from many, one; forever uniting, growing, dissolving—forever changing. The universe is God's self-portrait.

I am shaped by an impression of a contemplative life that invites faith deconstruction to precede discernment and engagement with

2. Audre Lorde, *Black Unicorn: Poems* (New York, W. W. Norton & Company, 1995), 94.

3. Octavia Butler, *Parable of the Sower* (New York: Grand Central Publishing, 2000), 315.

the sacred. Within this view, experience and imagination are placed in a dialogue that runs parallel to the origin stories we inherit from collectives. In a Christian context, the narrative of Jesus's birth begins with the person and symbolism of Mary. Mary, the fourteen-year-old encountering God's plans for her womb. Mary, betrothed and displaced from her home while still very much a child. Carrying her child. Mary, the wife, and Mary, the mother, and Mary, the mother of the son of God. Mary, the mother of a child she didn't get to raise, or watch grow old. Mary, known for reasons she did not devise much less consider. Mary, enshrined with her traumas narrated as God's plan to save us from ourselves.

The implications of a white Mary mothering a white Jesus occupy many wakeful and restless hours. The consequences of humanizing teenage Mary, a woman of color, a Black mother, and before that a Black child; a Black girl child whose whole life was defined by state violence and religious violence and a complicated relationship with God.

Mary's homeless, unprotected body converts birth into a symbol of Christ's divinity, but what about Mary's humanity? What about Mary's survivorship? What about Mary's body sovereignty? What about Mary's, and her husband's, and her child's ethic of consent?

I was a child brought up in church by two parents who related to both their families and their communities through their faith. Faith provided a shared language for setting priorities, for responding to loss or crisis, and for navigating how to engage in shared conversations with God as a couple. This was the constant amidst unending change, and that commitment was expressed daily. As a sibling to a sister with special needs, as a sibling to a sister with a heart condition, and as a daughter of someone dying from cancer, this parental orientation was passed on to me. It was passed on and internalized subtly, and it's only been as I've engaged in therapy as an adult that I've grown conscious of these persistent messages. I wear them in my DNA.

I wore them as a child experiencing sexual abuse, and later as a teenager. I wore them as a child in a blended family, the sibling and the child of people connected through intimacy with death. And I wear them as an adult who was pregnant at fourteen, now eighteen years later.

When something is a constant in your life, your orientation shifts to viewing it as familiar or absent in various settings and relationships. Does this person carry this message into the present? Does this history apply here? Are we able to communicate about what is unshared between us?

In a family that prayed together daily, I have no memories as a child learning about God with my parents or siblings. I can't recall how my parents talked about God—only that they did often. My ability to share my relationship with God was not nurtured or requested by my caregivers, only my proximity to church.

When I was a teenager, my widowed mother noticed specific signals and corrected them. If I appeared physically uncomfortable. If I was rude. If I kept my thoughts private. And if I said no to opportunities to serve. Service was the love language my mother cared about, the theology she practiced. It is the way she showed that, for her, faith was as straightforward as being present to your community's needs, with the caveat being that those needs are assumed known.

There's something deeply loving in this that I relate to as a love letter to my dad, but I feel alienated by the removal of nuance, the dismissal of inquiry, and the attunement to specific needs. There's little opportunity to build trust while performing your faith this way, alone with God together.

My grandmother was one of my favorite adults growing up, and she sought time alone with me. She taught me the importance of spending time with children in your personal space modeling immersion. Her daughters never met her parents because they died before she was married. Raised as a unitarian, my grandmother didn't grow up praying to Jesus, and I must say the way she related to me exuded less structured beliefs and habits of church. She was in my presence. She died on Father's Day as I finished my freshman year of high school. I was pregnant at the time, though I did not know it. I had experienced almost a decade of sexual violence already, and my narratives for choice and consent reflected a belief that violence couldn't be important if it was constant. It couldn't affect me, or my relationship with God, or my reaction to circling messages. At fourteen, I gave birth alone to a daughter that was conceived forcibly, and it is a truth that I did not want to carry or mother this child. It's a truth that I carried this child as one of thousands of secrets, just as I would this difficult and late-term miscarriage.

In my grief that felt like rage, for reasons void of motherly affection, I began asking questions about Mary before I could enter my own experience of God. Childhood messages surfaced as projected theology that kept me alienated from myself. I still know those theologies well and easily. Ones that frame a teenage girl's faith as bodily surrender to God. Ones that call that surrender consent and repeat that story to children over and over and over. Ones that make beautiful ballads as Mary's love songs to God. Ones that fail to consider that maybe ... Mary did love God and did not want to be Jesus's mother. Ones that use Mary's knowledge of God's activity in her world as a synonym for giving permission to incarnate the gospel in her. Ones that make Mary's life a blank slate before that angelic dialogue, a life that would have no influence on her response or the meanings she'd make afterwards. I'd love to talk to Mary age fifteen—and Mary age sixteen, and Mary repairing her trust in God even while serving.

My use of language for picturing and characterizing God has evolved as an adult in response to my experiences and frameworks that I have been provided with both in and out of church. Language is contextual, and an unfolding pandemic is at the center, influencing the structure of faith communities. Every word choice has to be more intentional. "Faith formation" is a term to describe the holistic development of faith supported by resources and relationships throughout one's whole life. Engaging spiritual education with this understanding has relational and theological consequences—and, in my experience, leads us toward our childhoods and our attitudes toward children. This reorientation is a part of a much broader theme in response to questions that both caregivers and church leaders are asking—about parenting, about grandparenting, about spiritual disciplines, about scripture, about group discernment, about inherited beliefs, about our lectionary, about interfaith dialogue, about generational differences, about represented leaders, as sociocultural context, and about anti-Blackness. This work has largely been led by those deconstructing their faith as adults, by women of color, by caregivers consciously rethinking their theology, and by our changing context for faith development. Considering children means considering family, pulling open endless drawers.

Households range from single parents, grandparents raising children, those who grew up in church and those who didn't or left on purpose, queer and gender nonconforming caregivers, those with trauma histories and varying politics, multifaith households. Intergenerational faith formation is both a reality and an aim because Church is a multigenerational community. Where intergenerational ministry differs is in embodying the goal for multiple generations to be present, contributing and adding value together, with the goal of teaching, modeling, and grounding this in a shared theological standpoint. This should not surprise us, because a simple conversation with a child about their bus ride or walk to school will expose the edges of homogeneity, the concepts they know by word if not meaning, and what isn't shared at all.

I remember a portrait sketched of me recently by a Black child and artist. They entitled it "flower child," and in place of facial features, they drew flower petals, in place of hair, roots and leaves of a tree. Alongside these words and this image, I recall the questions children have asked me in the last several weeks:

Do people need to have children?
How did you decide to become a parent?
Why are so many of my neighbors white?
Do you believe that all people are children of the universe?
Do you believe that all people are connected by Jesus?
Why aren't more Bibles written by women?
Why aren't there more stories of women?
How does this make you feel?
What does "out of reach" mean?
What is a human right?
Why are books banned?
Is this gaslighting?
What is your body saying to you?
What should we play?

Peer spaces and public spaces are quickly contradicting our whitewashing of them, and both our explanations and silence is being internalized. The censoring of ideas is kept in our news as headlines that sound like, "Another concerned parent wants this book out of their child's hands." Usually, the hypothetical child is in high school reading about addiction, enslavement, depression, a work written by a Black or trans author describing their lived experiences, or our wider lived experiences still avoided or belittled. I am perhaps most aware of this when I engage new translations of sacred texts from biblical scholars, and when I am teaching myself.

The Rev. Dr. Wil Gafney describes this much better than I can, in her introduction to *A Women's Lectionary for the Whole Church:*

> Biblical women are often generalized as a monolith of oppressed biblical womanhood. In my years teaching in theological classrooms and Jewish and Christian congregations, I find scripture readers unfamiliar with women prophets, or the more than twenty named Israelite and Judean queens preserved in the texts, or the female assassins who execute the would-be rapists, or many other texts in which women have unexpected power and agency. A significant aim of this project is increased biblical literacy, beginning with scripture's most neglected population.[4]

This was affirmed for me again most recently while I was teaching Confirmation to a class of middle school students. I asked the question, "Can you share with me any stories you remember in the Bible that include pregnancy?" I looked through the screen as the anxiety rose in their faces, next elaborating that the only story they could think of was Mary. I read them a story of Hagar, and Sarai, Elizabeth, Hannah, and Ruth, not wanting to shame them but to illuminate that there's more. Experiencing God is importantly plural, inclusive of meanings that are difficult to relate to even when we identify with a spoken encounter or dialogue with ourselves. What I understand at thirty-two that I did not at fourteen is that the archetypes we have and don't have for encountering God directly correlate with how we notice aspects of ourselves and our communities. Today my faith acknowledges that everything about God is laced with power dynamics, to a degree I didn't have language for as a child. These dynamics are made clearer when discussions about God avoid confronting this reality.

I have outlined this simply as two coexisting continuums highlighted in scripture—a continuum of God's activity across time

---

4. Wilda C. Gafney, *A Women's Lectionary for the Whole Church, Year W* (New York: Church Publishing, 2021), xiii.

and place as experienced and as observed, and a continuum of vio-lent activity as experienced and as observed. Both are intimately contextual and felt. Neither can be reduced, avoided, or made into anything else without distorting human experiences. And every time we distort lived experience, we change the nature of our relationship with God and ourselves. We change the very nature of how faith is internalized, and how self-trust is cultivated. We make trusting each other, and trusting our ability to be supported and cared for, harder to invest in.

During a car ride, my four-year-old niece asked to listen to the soundtrack from the musical *Rent*,[5] which she's never seen. As we drove and each song started, she would inquire, what's this song about? Who is singing? Who are they talking to— and what are they saying back? I engaged her questions as I clarified the lived experiences being discussed—chronic illness, death, gentri-fication, protest, gender and sexual identity, housing, capitalism, support system, relationships, addiction, collective action, com-munity safety. And what my niece came back to over and over is sources of care, and sources of vulnerability. What generated the experiences described, and what had the ability to change them and make them safer. Just from the music, she received that *Rent* is a narrative about friends acting on behalf of each other's safety, and those actions stem from a shared experience of gentrification and displacement as harmful. They were mobilized and informed by the shared beliefs that linked them, and their care for each other was something they each would rely on at different points. In this way, a value system emerges that is explicitly communicated and protected. Theology can be like this, but somehow our engagement with faith communities can conceal our beliefs about God—and if they're shared or not. Those seeds are lost when the questions we have in childhood are answered too simply or discouraged.

---

5. Jonathan Larson, *Rent* (New York: New York Theatre Workshop, 1996).

In December of 2020, I graduated from an accelerated master's program in Industrial Organizational Psychology and have not returned to institutional settings full time. I am a professional trained to diagnose organizational behavior and ambivalent about the right of institutions to exist. Increasingly, I am distrustful of institutional churches as conveners for faith formation. In both cases, this trend of skirting around accountability for stated beliefs influences my disengagement. I have experienced this pattern in crisis services, in child and youth development, in parenting, education and nonprofit cultures, in advocacy and mental health services, in activism and direct action. Each skill set I've added to my repertoire has reinforced a boundary I had been taught to diminish.

Poignantly, I wrote a statement of purpose for a PhD program I applied to centered on an ethos of consent in professional education. I described the pattern I still witness of crafting supplemental training programs to avoid the work of interrogating our working assumptions and what they've yielded, especially in terms of safety. I would describe this in consent education workshops as the part in learning where we think what we've learned can coexist with what we already believe, and not that it will change our beliefs to allow for new skills and connections to emerge. Our brain builds a new shelf instead of taking any books off.

In the last three years, I have been consciously preparing myself to be pregnant again by considering what could be different about choosing to parent, rather than connecting parenting to past assaults. And, as I have engaged in that self-work, I notice references to Mary that have failed to humanize her. I have had the benefit of eighteen years of conversations with God, regardless of a backdrop of violence. I have not remained in a conception of God, or a conception of God that I developed as a pregnant teenager, or as an abused child. I have not allowed my thirty-two-year-old self to extract my younger self's resilience to sustain or mature my faith formation. And I have not allowed caregiving to be my only identifier. I can recognize what non-consent sounds like within limited available language and projected meanings. I can empathize with needing those projected meanings to become soft-landing pads that anchor our sense of belonging. I know what disclosures have cost me, and what longings linger and expand as I permit myself to disclose anyway.

There is a context for God that exists alongside a context for violence that exists alongside a context for mothering that exists alongside a constant invitation to abandon bodies to speak their experiences and needs into voids with no listeners left. The listeners have moved on to the coming Christ child and the collective yearnings they believe have been validated finally. Maybe they have, and maybe an older Mary would profess that her needs were met through carrying Jesus. And yet, maybe Mary's faithfulness can't be reduced or externalized for us to inherit or validate. Maybe Christianity has cast too long of a shadow on Mary's experience and that is a testimony to observe. Maybe the lessons Jesus learned about consent emerged from observing his mother's traumas alongside her love for him. Maybe they were transformed through what coexisted and passed between them. Maybe our faith would change if we considered this as vital to our own formation and deconstruction.

My engagement with scripture is rooted in Mary, a Black mother whose birth story is rarely unpacked. My engagement with faith communities rejects any more invitations to leave my body to belong. My engagement with institutions is alerted to any unarticulated value systems. My engagement with children is conscious of power dynamics. My engagement with leadership is oriented to stated goals that direct how we practice what we want for each other. And it always includes safety. When we can externalize truths outside of our experiences, we can recognize the variables that cultivate collective action—and if we support them and want them as our inheritances. We can bring those longings forward and trust that we have the right to more safety with God and with each other. We can illuminate gaps and speak into them while trust forms slowly and translations come forward for our engagement.

I cannot tell you about Mary's rage, but I can tell you about my own. I can acknowledge my own commitment to deconstructing my faith and my experiences of violence in childhood. I can love a teenager whose context restricted how her faith was represented to her. I can love the language I have benefited from having, and the times before I had it and trusted myself. I can long to have relationships in faith communities that can hold changing self-understanding without sacrificing opportunities to depend on each other.

Full of humility, and my own rage and grief, I begin to engage with Mary—not as Christ's mother yet. Full of humility and released certitudes, I reengage Mary—never not Christ's mother, always herself. Always herself first—the body that birthed Jesus, the body that lived that experience, the body whose faith we have barely been invited to encounter or trust.

I marvel at Mary, the lover of God's justice, and Mary as an important teacher within my faith. I offer gratitude for the questions she provokes me to ask, and I pray to know her better. I pray to know her as she knows herself, and all the selves she may have evolved into. I pray to choose faith practices that dream of more safety for all of us. I pray to only engage in faith formation that links me more honestly to real people's well-being.

Under Books

My babies will be cradled among bookcases.
They will know lullabies of poetry and speak poets' names . . .
Alice Walker, Kahlil Gibran, Audre Lorde, Rumi, Annie Dillard,
Rita Dove, Maggie Smith, Ocean Vuong, Warsan Shire, Hafiz.
Their lips will sing out with the color purple, raptured by a God
more beautiful than all our stories of them.
They will trust Black women and I hope themselves.

They will not be a rib pulled from any illusion of a cage, even the one that protected these lungs, and this heart.

I will not claim them within my essence, nor keep mine from them.

I will let their sleep involve stirring, rolling around with eyes opened by dazzling darkness and the flicker of contact with the universe.

I will give them the words I have. . . .

You are safe with me.

Your wisdom dazzles me.

Your joy astounds my trauma and opens my imagination to God.

God, the midwife and not the conquistador.

God, the hue and not the sensation.

God, the paint and not the artist.

God, the art.

You the art.

Your dreams witnessed by just enough light to read to as I sing us to sleep. . . .

hey sister whatcha gonna do? Goin' down by the river gonna play with you.[6]

We don't always pray our words; sometimes we pray by listening to the cellular, overwhelming ballads.

The ones children sang first to themselves and their visions.[7]

6. Lyric from "Our Prayer," *The Color Purple*, music and lyrics by Brenda Russell, Allee Willis, and Stephen Bray, CD, 2006.

7. Amanda Lindwood, "Under the Books," 2022.

8

To Heal What Ails Us

Belonging through
Group Spiritual Direction

Melanie Dobson

An Experience of Belonging

The midmorning summer light shone golden and warm just outside the shadows of the covered deck at Bon Secours Retreat Center. A circle of four wise women, with listening skills honed by their lives as clergy and therapists, sat with me on the plush cushions of the outdoor wicker furniture. The program director had just finished teaching our cohort in Shalem's Spiritual Guidance program about group spiritual direction. Now it was our turn to practice, and it was my turn to share. I had five minutes to talk about God's presence in my life.

I took a deep breath, and with the exhale, began pulling at the thread to start unraveling my story. I felt a hard knot of anxiety that felt stuck in my ribcage, making it hard to exhale evenly. I began: "I feel so stuck in my work as a pastor. I sense God is calling me into a new vocation and I'm scared and fearful. As I look to the fall during which I will have to make some decisions, the future feels like this vast unknown. I will need such courage to make a change into what doesn't even exist yet. God's voice in all this feels unclear—mostly because I'm staying too busy to hear. I'm overwhelmed and unsure—and exhausted."

I began feeling teary. The unspooling of the knot seemed to bring with it the unraveling of some tied-up emotion too. I felt the women in the circle gaze at me with love. We moved into two minutes of silence—during which I largely tried not to sniffle or ugly cry. Silence can be a space of my undoing.

A group member gently pulled us out of the silence and invited us into a time of responses. I honestly don't remember a single thing that anyone said in that ten-minute time. I can't report any of their thoughtful words or insightful glimpses into the heart of the Holy—though I'm sure the words were gems. I do remember an extraordinary feeling of compassion from the circle. I felt held by their warmth and love, the rays of which resembled the summer sunshine just beyond us. I remember feeling nestled in the loving language of prayer that was just for me. It was a profound experience of belonging to God and to wise friends. In their caring attention I received what I needed but couldn't articulate—a spirit of strength for whatever was before me and a deep knowing that I wasn't alone. That spirit was enough to finish unraveling the knot until I finally felt my whole chest cavity free and soft for the first time in months.

The group held me in silent prayer while the next person in the circle was given their allotted twenty-minute time. I listened and offered my heart to them in the Holy Spirit, as they had offered themselves to me. The thread of connection, unspooled, connected our hearts to each other. If it is possible to fall in love with a practice, I did on that warm summer morning in those wicker chairs. I fell hard for group spiritual direction—for the healing, for the connection, and for the spirit of belonging.

We Are Lonely

Why did I need that circle so much? I needed that practice of group spiritual direction because I felt alone. Honestly, perhaps the truthful word is—lonely. If loneliness is defined as "the sub-jective feeling that you're lacking the social connections you need and missing the feeling of closeness, trust, and affection of genu-ine friends and loved ones"—then that describes my feeling.[1] I felt isolated in these large life decisions before me. An outsider looking at my life wouldn't readily see my sensed lack of social connection, which is why loneliness is so subjective.

As a clergyperson in a large church, I was constantly sur-rounded by people—tons of people—all the time. Our office space buzzed with visits from parishioners and community members, not to mention the over fifty-plus staff people with whom I inter-acted daily. With my parishioners I felt real love and connection, but there was an invisible boundary. I listened, I taught, I shared enough of my story for connection, but I did not share my full vulnerability. I needed to remain their pastor. Rare were spaces in which I could freely divulge my deepest heart concerns. Find-ing time for heartful connections was rare as well—life as a single clergy mom didn't allow lots of space for nurturing friendships—or I did not prioritize it over the tyranny of the urgent in my sense of work. Amid difficult decisions of vocation, I was so hungry for a community in which I could fully be heard and belong—and wasn't in the role of a supervisor, pastor, teacher, or spiritual direc-tor. That circle on that sunny veranda gave me a dose of connec-tion that I did not even fully realize I was missing. I didn't know the extent of my loneliness until I felt the antidote—a profound sense of belonging in a circle of loving people with whom I had no other role than friend.

It turns out that I am not alone in my feeling of loneliness or lack of belonging. Surgeon General Vivek Murthy, in referring to a 2018 report from the Henry J. Kaiser Foundation, writes that the

---

1. Vivek Murthy, *Together: The Healing Power of Connection in a Sometimes Lonely World* (New York: Harper Wave, 202), 8.

longing for human connection while feeling its absence has become pervasive in American culture. He goes on to state that prior to the Covid-19 pandemic, 22 percent of adults said they felt lonely or socially isolated, with one in three over the age of forty-five feeling lonely.[2] After the pandemic, close to 40 percent of Americans feel lonely frequently or almost all of the time. Feelings of isolation and disconnection are particularly pervasive among the hyper-social-media-connected young: over 60 percent of young adults indicated that they feel lonely and that no one in the past few weeks has taken the time to ask how they are doing or to express genuine care for them. Moms with young children also feel incredibly isolated, struggling with exhaustion and loneliness while engaged in the never-ending daily care of babies and toddlers.[3]

Loneliness can have different dimensions too. The loneliness I felt was a yearning for quality friendships and social companionship, which is called relational/social loneliness. Intimate loneliness is a longing for a close confidant or intimate partner with whom you share a deep mutual bond of affection and trust. Collective loneliness is the hunger for a community of people who share a sense of purpose and interests. These three dimensions of loneliness can be experienced in any combination in any human in a given time; we need all three of these longings satisfied in order to survive and thrive. The lack of any one of them can create loneliness. The moms with young children might have an intimate partner but lack a collective connection. The lonely young adults might have social connections but lack a close confidante. The complexity of the dimensions of loneliness in our disconnected culture creates a high likelihood that any one of us at any given time is experiencing loneliness of some sort.

---

2. Murthy, *Together*, 10.

3. "Loneliness in America: How the Pandemic Has Deepened Loneliness and What We Can Do About It," Making Caring Common Project, Harvard University, February 9, 2021, https://mcc.gse.harvard.edu/reports/loneliness-in-america.

"Loneliness hangs over our culture today like a thick smog," states Johann Hari in his profound book, *Lost Connections: Why You're Depressed and How to Find Hope.*[4] Americans increasingly live isolated lives, with plummeting involvement in community groups, church, sports leagues, and social gatherings. Neighborhoods lack cohesion; people do not gather on front porches and kids don't play pick-up games in their street. We also are not gathering with people in our own household. Families are not eating, playing, or even watching TV together as much as they did prior to the turn of the twenty-first century.[5] Even while under the same roof, people stare at their phone screens and eat meals in different rooms. This inward turn is also reflected in the number of close friends people have—or don't. The number with whom people feel safe sharing their most vulnerable stories has dropped from three people several decades ago to none by the early 2000s.[6] We live our lives increasingly alone.

After my amazing experience of belonging in group spiritual direction on a sunny porch, I began wondering about loneliness. I wanted to know why I—and so many others—are so lonely. I wondered about the impact of loneliness on my own and everyone else's physical, mental, and emotional health. I also wondered how the practice of group spiritual direction might be the prescription for what we most need—belonging. These three open-ended questions served as a form of spiritual direction for me. In a culture of epidemic loneliness, the practice of group spiritual direction provides spaces of belonging for which people so desperately need and

---

4. Johann Hari, *Lost Connections: Why You're Depressed and How to Find Hope* (New York: Bloomsbury, 2019), 79.

5. Robert Putnam, *Bowling Alone: The Collapse and Revival of American Community* (New York: Simon and Schuster, 2001), 111–12. Putnam's well-known study, now a couple of decades old, explored trends of increasing isolation that have only increased since then. See more recent social science work by John Cacioppo and William Patrick, *Loneliness: Human Nature and the Need for Social Connection* (New York: W. W. Norton, 2008).

6. Hari, *Lost Connections*, 80.

long. Group spiritual direction might just be a way that God uses to save us from our loneliness and isolation.

Question 1: Why Are We So Lonely?

1. Capitalist Economy

Our cultural economy is built on making money or status—and always staying busy. The European descent (White) culture exerts enormous pressure on us to be productive. The father of capitalism, Adam Smith, intended in his 1776 foundational economic text *An Inquiry into the Nature and Causes of the Wealth of Nations* to create a system that engages self-interest in order to move goods through the division of labor.[7] Sadly the focus on both self-interest and commodities led to a focus on stuff as the way we satisfy our desires—and endless labor as the way we procure that stuff. This economics of scarcity teaches us that we are not enough, that we do not have enough money, that we don't have enough stuff—so that we will keep working to get more money and buy more stuff to purchase status and self-worth. This economics of deformation becomes its own form of oppression.[8] We live in a system of capitalism that values us as human beings based on our productivity and income generation, rather than in our innate value as made in the image of God. Tragically, the more our lives focus on work, stuff, and status, the more lonely, depressed, and isolated we become.[9]

Even beyond idolatrous materialism, extractive capitalism warps us so that success and achievement become a measure of our worth—even in faith communities. Proeschold-Bell and Byassee write about how clergy struggle under the burden to demonstrate "church vitality" and the stress of pastoring to show "success" in

---

7. Adam Smith, *The Wealth of Nations* (New York: Penguin Classics, 1982).
8. Hari, *Lost Connections*, 100.
9. Hari, *Lost Connections*, 96.

ministry resulting in overworking and productivity, not generally because of income, but because it indicates our own value, faithfulness to God (what a heavy burden!), and commitment to our calling.[10] As a clergyperson, I felt the pressure to grow ministries and programs. I confess that even as I was immersed in the ministry of forming small groups for others to connect, I did not allow enough space for myself to do so. The daily and weekly grind of serving in the church and my own devotion to this 24/7 work kept me from making space to replenish myself with meaningful and profound human connection. I did have a monthly gathering with a small group of clergywomen sisters, who met at my home on Fridays for lunch and a contemplative practice of reading scripture called *lectio divina*. This was a significant time of community—but I also knew they were busy pastoring churches and parenting kids, working just as hard as I was. I did not want to "bother" them with my own needs outside of our monthly meeting time—even though I intrinsically knew they would be more than happy to be present to me. The culture pressed upon me to be productive, and for my friends to be productive, so that creating space to actually connect and make room for what we most needed—deep friendship—felt absolutely countercultural and difficult to schedule.

2. Cult of Individualism

Even more, our Western/American culture's affirmation of the individual as the source of all capacity exacerbates the intensity of the work/materialism drive. Immanuel Kant, a philosopher from the 1700s, offered the insight that we can turn inward to our own consciousness to know how to act ethically. However, this inward turn sowed the seeds of self-reliance, which turns out to be false. We

---

10. Rae Jean Proeschold-Bell and Jason Byassee, *Faithful and Fractured: Responding to the Clergy Health Crisis* (Grand Rapids: Baker Academic, 2018) documents all the ways that clergy struggle under the burden to demonstrate church "vitality" and the stress of pastoring to show "success" in ministry.

cannot do things on our own. We cannot pull ourselves up by our own bootstraps. We can't even feed, clothe, or shelter ourselves on our own. We need each other as humans, not only to satisfy our physical needs, but our emotional ones too—which are just as important. Yet, our Western culture tells us, "Fix your loneliness yourself. See a doctor. Go on drugs. Get a therapist. You can do it! All by yourself!" While therapy and medications can do us good, adhering to self-improvement and self-help prescriptions leaves us feeling frustrated at best, and really lonely at worst. An individualistic focus on self-help to fix loneliness generates its own form of isolation.

3. Transience

Global capitalism also contributes to constant human migration. Work opportunities, the drive for education for better economic improvement, climate change, economic crises, and immigration leads to an overall cultural uprootedness. We move to take better jobs (there's the impact of capitalism!), to seek out education for our children, to have safety—we are a globe of humans in constant movement.[11] As a result, we land in places apart from family, friends, social networks, or any kind of supportive community. Without any rootedness in communities of human connection and love, transplants and immigrants feel the weight of loneliness and often struggle with mental health issues related to loneliness and depression.[12]

4. Privileged and White Culture

This strong form of both extractive capitalism and excessive individualism has its taproot in White European and European-descent culture. Thinkers such as Adam Smith and Immanuel Kant

---

11. Murthy, *Together*, 127. Close to 4 percent of the world's population lived outside their home countries in 2019, while close to 70 million adults plan movement because of persecution, war, or violence. Another 18 million people in 135 countries were displaced by weather related disasters in 2017.

12. Murthy, *Together*, 125–27.

contributed to the ideological formation of this culture; John Locke added to this intellectual canon the pursuit and protection of "private" property. The expansive impact of colonialism, in which land became something for Europeans to possess, own, and extract resources from, laid the foundation for a brutal capitalism in which power, domination, and wealth were pursed at great costs to creation and creatures. Having a sense of place in the land and in all its living things became replaced by a relentless pursuit of profits—profits derived from the brutal enslavement of other human beings and from extracting from the land all its resources and strength.[13] The gathering of people became for greed instead of for belonging—from the hoarding of people on the slave ship, to the plantation, to the field—to harness communal action for conquest and for power.[14]

The result of this brutal capitalism and individualism is the production of displacement.[15] One place is just as good as another to live, make money, and buy the same stuff—the same box stores hulk on parking lots from sea to shining sea. Neighborhoods built on private property stretch for miles of suburban sameness, with separate driveways and often gates at the front to keep community out. This capitalist neighborhood planning leads to empty streets and to neighbors who do not know each other, and who do not ask each other for support and help.

This landscape contributes to churches in which people cannot or do not know how to be vulnerable. Church prayer requests include cancer diagnoses but not any admittances that a person may feel depressed, or terribly lonely—because to admit that would be an admittance of failure of not living up to one's success and achievement. It is a desperate and isolated place to be—to not know that

---

13. Matthew Desmond, "Capitalism," in *The 1619 Project: A New Origin Story*, created by Hannah Nikole-Jones (New York: One World Publishing, 2021).

14. Willie Jennings, *After Whiteness: An Education in Belonging* (Grand Rapids: Eerdmans, 2019), 135–36.

15. Willie Jennings, "The Geography of Whiteness," interview by Matthew Vega, *Christian Century*, November 2, 2021, 26.

you are deeply loved for who you are, as you are. To live in privilege is to lack places of true belonging. It is to be displaced from one's soul's greatest needs and from any chance at real, vulnerable community. Ironically, faith communities can perpetuate the very experiences of isolation and exclusion that they ought to be obviating.

The profound culture of sickness embedded in the very ground of our culture—in our stripped topsoil, polluted waterways, sprawling shopping malls, and isolated houses built on the shrine of private property—poisons White people and kills Black, Asian, Indigenous, and Latin peoples because of its power.[16] The chronic condition of loneliness stems from generations of a world "being stolen, privatized, segmented, segregated, commoditized, and bordered."[17] We dwell isolated from each other. The devastating impact of this is that we are literally collectively unwell . . . sick in our own isolated bedrooms while staring at screens, longing to be seen and heard. When not at home alone, we work ourselves to death. Yet inside, we are empty and dark, dying of loneliness from the separation, competition, and individualism. Our deep soul struggle is for communion and connection.

5. Shame

The loneliness brings along with it the burden of shame. When people feel lonely and see others having fun together, especially on social media, they tend to withdraw even more, exacerbating the situation. They might feel like a social outcast. Shame and fear become a self-perpetuating condition, as increasing self-doubt and lower self-esteem contribute to further isolation and withdrawal. Instead of turning to others for a connection that can help, people turn to alcohol, drugs, food, or sex to numb the emotional pain. The stigma of loneliness exacerbates it and causes great harm to personal and

---

16. Jennings, *After Whiteness*, 140.
17. Jennings, *After Whiteness*, 136.

collective health.[18] However, loneliness is simply the natural emotional signal that we all need connection with other people. This desire for connection is as innate as the desire for food or drink when we are hungry or thirsty. There is no shame in the need for connection, and there should be no stigma for loneliness. We need human relationships of depth and meaning to survive and thrive.[19]

6. The Use of Social Media

To satisfy the need for human connection in a world in which we cannot admit that need for shame, people turn to their phones and the apps on them. We are online, all the time. We check them obsessively, dwelling on our devices for hours a day, seeking "likes" and updating our status within sophisticated technology designed to addict us and which is increasingly harming us.[20] We are seeking acknowledgment, connection, and relationship from a cyberspace that cannot satisfy the depths of our embodied longings, ultimately leading to a greater feeling of disconnection.[21] Or, as theologians Craig Van Gelder and Dwight Zschiele put it, "The paradox of a technologically interlinked society is increasing aloneness."[22] When used as a sole destination for connection, however, social media leaves people feeling more distant, alone, and lessened by comparison.[23]

Humans need face-to-face, in-person encounters in which we see, smell, hear, and touch each other in spaces where we feel

---

18. Murthy, *Together*, 11.
19. Murthy, *Together*, 11.
20. Murthy, *Together*, 102. Murthy cites studies which show that heavy use of social media contributes to feelings of loneliness and depression. He also indicates that social media uses human behavior science combined with software engineering to keep us on the apps and to keep bringing us back. The more time we spend on the app, the more money social media makes in the new "attention" economy (105).
21. Murthy, *Together*, 111.
22. Craig Van Gelder and Dwight Zschiele, *Participating in God's Mission: A Theological Missiology for the Church in America* (Grand Rapids: Eerdmans, 2018), 243.
23. Murthy, *Together*, 114.

cared for and loved. Screens cannot mediate that embodied, incarnate experience of belonging.[24] As neuroscience researcher John Cacioppo stated, "Social media can't compensate us psychologically for what we have lost—social life."[25] Friendships and relationships developed online or through networking services tend to be more conditional and lack the time, attention, and effort that friendship really requires.[26] We may have more online connections, but they do not have the same meaning or emotional sustenance that embodied friendships do, according to Stanford sociology professor Dr. Paolo Parigi. The real practice of presence, of being heard and understood, is often missing from more superficial online interactions.

Taken together, the impact of brutal capitalism, individualism, transiency, and shame leaves people profoundly lonely and unable to talk about it. More than those feelings, loneliness actually does have a somatic effect and profound implications for their health. My tied-up knot of anxiety that I felt on the day I first practiced group spiritual direction came from loneliness, but I was not even able to identify the source at the time. If left untreated, that knot could have detrimental effects on every aspect of my health and well-being. I wondered about the overall health impacts of loneliness . . . which led me to explore the second question.

Question 2: How Is Loneliness Harming Us. . . and How Belonging Heals Us

Created for Connection

We were not made to be alone. We were made for connection. God created us to belong in life together with God, one another, and all creation. As embodied creatures we are formed to share, taste,

---

24. Hari, *Lost Connections*, 88–89.
25. Hari, *Lost Connections*, 89.
26. Murthy, *Together*, 109. Murthy uses the research of Parigi and MIT professor Sherry Turkle to cite research on the difference between online and in-person relationships.

touch, see, hear the goodness of God in one another as members of a community.[27] We literally need belonging in order to survive: "Human relationship is as essential to our well-being as food and water."[28]

As creatures vulnerable to elements and to predators, the earliest humans survived through community and cooperation in tribes. By hunting, farming, caring for young, and fending off threats together, humans managed to sustain life. As neuroscience researcher John Cacioppo puts it, "Against harsh odds humans barely survive, but the fact that they survive at all they owe to the dense web of social contacts and the vast number of reciprocal commitments they maintain. In this state of nature, connection and social co-operation did not have to be imposed ... nature is connection."[29] Loneliness, then, was not survivable for the earliest humans, but is rather "an aversive state that motivates us to reconnect."[30]

Anxiety, Depression, and Premature Mortality from Loneliness

We feel anxious and insecure when we don't have connection. We do not feel

safe. Our embodied selves understand at a cellular level that we can't survive loneliness. We are wired to feel afraid and poor in isolation—which is why solitary confinement remains the worst form of torture and incarceration. Loneliness, therefore, heightens anxiety. Exploding rates of anxiety in our culture and especially in our young are directly attributable to how we live now—frantically busy, isolated, and alone.[31]

---

27. Jennings, *After Whiteness*, 11.
28. Murthy, *Together*, 11.
29. Cacioppo and William, *Loneliness*, 61.
30. Hari, *Lost Connections*, 78.
31. "Loneliness in America," https://mcc.gse.harvard.edu/reports/loneliness-in-america. Over 65 percent of young adults report feeling anxious and depressed.

Not only does loneliness foster anxiety, but it also leads to depression. Research now reveals that loneliness is a prime causation of depression. Experiences of belonging and connection radically lessened people's experience of depression.[32]

Even more significant, loneliness contributes to premature mortality. Health and social psychology researcher Dr. Julianne Holt-Lunstad's comprehensive studies on social relationships found that people with weak social connections were 50 percent more likely to die prematurely than people with strong social connections, and demonstrated a correlation between loneliness and heart disease, high blood pressure, stroke, dementia, depression, and anxiety.[33] Loneliness and lack of social connection creates a risk equal to smoking fifteen cigarettes a day and is a greater risk to life span than obesity, sedentary lifestyle, or excess alcohol consumption.[34] We are literally killing ourselves with loneliness.[35]

The tight wound-up feeling I had in my chest as I came to my first experience of group spiritual direction represented stress. I was worried about my future and about my vocational direction. What I did not realize was that I also felt lonely in this huge life discernment. The time in loving community unwound that tight ball. Connection in that circle of loving support was the prescription I did not even know I needed.

Belonging: Medical, Psychological, and Social Benefits

Increasingly, practitioners of Western medicine recognize the significance of people's emotional and social health, and that humans

---

32. Hari, *Lost Connections*, 76.

33. Julianne Holt-Lunstad, Timothy Smith, and J. Bradley Layton, "Social Relationships and Mortality Risk: A Meta-Analytic Review," *PLOS. Medicine* 7, no. 7 (July 2010), https://doi.org/10.1371/journal.pmed.1000316.

34. Murthy, *Together*, 13.

35. Hari, *Lost Connections*, citing Susan Pinker, *The Village Effect: Why Face-to-Face Contact Matters (Toronto: Random House Canada, 2014)*, 282.

need more than pills to fix the loneliness that ails us. Chemical antidepressants may work for treating depression in some people, but the better treatment is human relationships.[36] Loneliness is a human condition that requires the consistent steady love, companionship, and compassion of fellow human beings, rather than an individual prescription for a drug or a surgical procedure.[37] These social prescriptions affirm the universal human need for connection as an essential aspect of not only emotional, but physical and mental health as well. Belonging with others in settings in which we feel loved heals us, whereas pills and medical interventions can fail us at times.[38]

It's not just joining a group—healing from belonging comes when there is a shared story, meaning, and experience. You can be with people and still feel alone in a group; my experience of being surrounded by so many people in my church work yet still feeling loneliness is a perfect example. There must be intentional forms of storytelling and contribution to a larger purpose or meaning for people to experience the benefits of human connection. You have to feel like you are sharing something that matters with others in order for loneliness to abate.[39]

In additional to medical science, social scientists now also confirm the power of belonging for healing. In sociologist Brené Brown's words, "We are psychologically, emotionally, cognitively, and spiritually hardwired for connection, love and belonging.

---

36. Hari, *Lost Connections*, 182–83. Hari notes that drugs can be helpful for some people, but the actual results of the clinical trials of antidepressant medications prove that their benefits are really small (35).

37. Murthy, *Together*, 16; Hari, *Lost Connections*, 197. For example, doctors at the clinic Bromley-by-Bow center in England sit alongside patients and ask (instead of what's the matter with you) "what matters to you?" Based upon that patient's answer, the doctor offers "social prescribing," which is a referral to social or community programs that align with the patient's own needs, desires, and hungers for connection.

38. Murthy, *Together*, 22.

39. Hari, *Lost Connections*, 83. Superficiality at a dinner party can contribute to loneliness, because you're with people but don't have any sense of connection to them.

Connection, along with love and belonging, is why we are here, and it is what gives purpose and meaning to our lives."[40] Being accepted fully for who we are happens when we share our life stories with each other. According to Vivek Murthy, "We are wired to associate belonging with the sharing of stories, feelings, memories, and concerns. The stories give meaning to our struggles, comfort us in times of suffering, and bond us."[41] The strong emotional connections add joy and meaning to our lives and buffer life's stresses, giving us the capacity to better weather life's challenges, whether illness, loss, or change.

Group spiritual direction provides a circle of connection in which we tell our life stories, and are fully accepted for who we are, as we are—it is a space of belonging that develops true friendship. Even more, in group spiritual direction, we offer ourselves for one another. Medical research demonstrates that doing something for others lifts anxiety and depression. Even if a person is in pain and struggling, connecting to someone else in a way that contributes to that person's life enhances mental health and well-being.[42] Though American individualistic culture teaches that the individual can pursue happiness, the wiser truth is that we experience health, wellness, and happiness collectively; when we work to make things better for a group we are elevated too: "Prosocial behavior, like helping others, leaves people feeling less anxious and threatened and more secure. . . . We are biologically primed to feel better together."[43] Serving others serves our own health and well-being

---

40. Brené Brown, *Daring Greatly* (Penguin Random House: New York, 2012), 68.

41. Murthy, *Together*, 32–33. Murthy goes on to detail the hormones and neurotransmitters in the body such as oxytocin, dopamine, and endorphins that release when we feel connection, or promote us to seek connection when we feel lonely.

42. Hari, *Lost Connections*, 183.

43. Murthy, *Together*, 33–34. Both Johann Hari and Vivek Murthy in their recent books on the healing power of belonging look to Christian communities as exemplars. Hari visits an Old Order Amish community and writes on their profound webs of connection. Murthy references the Quaker Parker Palmer's work of "circles of trust" as a practice for storytelling in circles of listening that tender belonging, community, and wellness.

too. In group spiritual direction, we offer our own hearts, minds, and souls on behalf of another's discernment and well-being; we give, and in so doing, receive benefits for our own spiritual, mental, and emotional health—and healing from whatever loneliness might ail us.

Sadly, many of our churches and faith communities, in striving for a kind of capitalist success narrative through extensive programming and a focus on numerical growth (even in decline), have forgotten that belonging happens in smallness—and that the healing power of belonging happens in tiny communities in which we are deeply known and loved. Scholars of Christian mission offer this analysis: "The hunger for community remains, but people leave the church in part because the church isn't addressing it."[44] Even the church members who remain can experience their own community as disconnected from the primary challenges people are facing in daily life, as organizational, administrative, or political agendas consume all the time—leaving little space for people to engage in authentic conversation about what matters to them.[45]

Question 3: How Group Spiritual Direction Provides the Balm of Healing Community

Group spiritual direction offers one way that we can offer real community and belonging—and in so doing, heal. Group spiritual direction invites us all to satisfy our deepest hungers for connection and contribution to the lives of others through circles of belonging. It is what the doctor ordered. For exhausted moms and lonely young adults, for those who just moved into a new city, for people on their screens seeking out community but feeling ever more

---

44. Craig Van Gelder and Dwight Zscheile, *Participating in God's Mission* (Columbus, OH: Ermans, 2018), 229.

45. Robert Wuthnow, *The Crisis in the Churches: Spiritual Malaise, Fiscal Woe* (New York: Oxford University Press, 1997). Wuthnow did research on middle-class churches and found this to be true.

alone as they wade through "likes" and virtual hugs, group spiritual direction can be the balm that our bodies, minds, and spirits so desperately need. If the social prescription for loneliness, anxiety, and depression is a community in which you share deeply and have deeper purpose, group spiritual direction offers that. It is a sanctuary of belonging—a place where the sunlight of empathy and of caring presence shines.

In the midst of the coronavirus pandemic, I felt the Spirit leading me to offer group spiritual direction for United Methodist clergywomen in my area. My fellow clergy were exhausted and overwhelmed by the ongoing pandemic and all the adaptations they had to make in ministry and in their personal lives. As a clergywoman myself, I felt an empathy with my fellow sisters and wanted to offer them group spiritual direction as a source of solace, restoration, and healing. Since gathering in person wasn't safe due to possibilities of contagion from Covid-19, I organized the practice over Zoom. Once a month on Friday afternoons we gathered in the Zoom space for an entire school year, from September to May.

When the monthly time for the group spiritual direction came, I never felt that I had the time for it. Part of me—even as the leader and a firm believer in the healing benefits of group spiritual direction—wanted to squirm out of it; there were always so many other things that felt pressing to do. Laundry still sat in the washer that I had not put in the dryer and dishes piled up in the sink, not to mention never-ending e-mail and work tasks. I was often not a calm pool of centered peace before I facilitated the group. My son practicing trumpet for his band class in the dining room probably didn't help. I felt stress about the hour and a half in which I could be getting other things done. A knot had lodged itself inside my chest yet again.

Nonetheless, I put myself in front of my computer screen and web camera and clicked into Zoom. I lit a candle and welcomed the small group of five women as they came into their Zoom squares. We said "hello" to each other and introduced ourselves. For the first few sessions, I offered a short teaching time on the group spiritual direction, using PowerPoint slides to orient them to the practice.

After a short time of silence, I moved us into the practice. By this point, I had forgotten about the laundry, and settled into listening. I felt my shoulders soften down from my ears. My breath deepened. One of my clergy siblings began sharing her anxiety because of a potential new appointment to a different church, and the added stresses of moving during Covid. She shared courageously of her trust in God, even if she did not fully trust the appointment process. In the time of offering responses, we lifted up the light that shone out from her, even in the unknown. We closed in silent prayer for trust in a liminal space.

As the listening, sharing, and silence moved around the Zoom space, we connected to each other. As my clergy sisters shared their stories and their struggles, we named each other's courage, heart, and strength to be human. The light that shone in them brought illumination to my own dark corners. If grief weighed heavy for one person, the group held it and alleviated the burden of grieving alone. We gave to one another new ways of seeing and interpreting our lives through the Holy Spirit. This way of belonging to each other gave meaning to our lives and greater well-being. It is a thread of connection that wove our hearts together.

At the end of every group spiritual direction session, as I click out of the Zoom or physically leave a circle, I'm reminded that this kind of sharing and belonging is what life is all about. Being with each other in life-giving relationships is why we are here. I've got all the time in the world for that. In fact, I need it for my own survival. A community of human and divine connection can unravel even the forces of capitalism, Whiteness, and shame—and its attendant forces of loneliness. Whatever might have been knitting a knot of stress or anxiety before the meeting gets unspooled by the power of the Holy Spirit at work among and through the people in the circle. My chest cavity is free and soft again. Even more I'm strengthened in the Spirit to move into what is before me with greater peace. Group spiritual direction gives me all these gifts—connection, belonging, meaning, relationships, and peace. I keep falling in love with this practice because it never fails to show me what matters most in this life—which is love of God and others. And love always heals.

Part 2

Holy Awe

At Shalem, we invite people into a space where they can practice and explore divine mystery at any given time in their lives. There is a lot of unknowing, which can at times be uncomfortable if you are one who is more tethered to maps, facts, and data. But as Meister Eckhart wrote: "There is a journey you must take. It is a journey without destination. There is no map. Your soul will lead you."[1]

While there is no blueprint for this journey, there are contemplative practices that have evolved throughout the wisdom of the ages and serve as a guide for experiencing the Holy Awe of Presence. And this "presence cannot be defined; it can only be experienced."[2]

There are so many things that can get in the way of seeing the sacred and the Holy in this shifting world today. But if you can allow space for the Holy Surprise, you might be able to experience the ultimate beauty of the Holy Awe. It will be in the small, seemingly insignificant encounters that will allow your soul to guide you. As rabbi, theologian, and philosopher Abraham Joshua Heschel wrote, "Awe enables us to perceive in the world intimations of the divine, to sense in small things the beginning of infinite significance, to sense the ultimate in the common and

---

1. Jon M. Sweeney and Mark S. Burrows, *Meister Eckhart's Book of the Heart: Meditations for the Restless Soul* (Charlottesville, WV: Hampton Roads, 2017), 166.
2. Richard Rohr, "Be Present as a Child," Center for Action and Contemplation, March 20, 2023, https://cac.org/daily-meditations/be-present-as-a-child-2023-03-20/.

the simple; to feel in the rush of the passing the stillness of the eternal."[3]

In part two, you are invited to journey with others as they experience the Holy Awe. In the first essay in this section, Westina Matthews reminds us that there are thousands of ways to experience the Holy Awe in contemplative living and leadership. We believe that this Presence can be experienced in the simple and small ways, and that you too can know the Holy Awe whether you believe in God, or Allah, or Buddha, or Jehovah, or Prophet Mohammed, or Spirit, or the Divine Goddess.

---

3. A. J. Heschel, *God in Search of Man* (New York: Farrar, Straus and Giroux, 1955), 75.

9

A Thousand Paths to Contemplation

Westina Matthews

The 2022 lecturer for the Gerald May Seminar was the Most Reverend Michael B. Curry who leads the U.S.-based Episcopal Church as presiding bishop. As the 27th presiding bishop, he is the first person of color—and African American—to serve in this role.

During the seminar, Curry said more than once, "I am not a contemplative." Yet, there was a moment when he broke out in song with "There Is a Balm in Gilead," a traditional African American hymn. Without hesitation, those of us who were in the audience began to join in, our eyes closing and our bodies swaying.

That was a contemplative moment.

For so many, contemplation brings up images of the Desert Mothers and Fathers who intentionally lived in solitude in order to commune with the Holy One; or perhaps others think of classical authors who described contemplative spirituality as a particular experience. Spiritual writer and Franciscan friar Richard Rohr reminds us that "contemplation is simply openness to God's loving presence in 'what is' right in front of you. . . . This presence to Presence can be cultivated in many ways that don't require sitting on a mat for twenty minutes."[1]

As an adult contemplative, I often hear the sixteenth-century mystic Thomas Keating's interpretation that "silence is God's first language."[2] But one of the first Bible verses that I learned in Sunday school was "Be still, and know that I am God" (Ps. 46:10, NIV). And might we also consider Howard Thurman, the African American theologian and scholar, who so eloquently wrote about "how good it is to center down"[3] an expansive invitation to stillness that may or may not include silence?

For contemplatives, there are many different ways to experience an interior life with God. I believe that there is no hierarchy in how one centers down, no preferred way over another. One can experience centering down through both silence and through stillness. As Joan Chittister reminds us: "Contemplation breaks us open to ourselves."[4] It is in that breaking open to ourselves to be present in the presence of God that I, as a contemplative, seek. Yet, as an African American, I sometimes feel constrained to more traditional contemplative practices that do not come out of my own faith walk which, in turn, creates a resistance deep within my soul to the very holy listening that I am seeking.

My own faith journey has been intentionally inclusive and was influenced greatly by my parents. When I arrived on the college campus (a Catholic institution) my freshman year, I was asked repeatedly by students and faculty: "Are you Catholic?" When I replied that I was Methodist, I was told that I did not drink,

---

1. Richard Rohr, "Conscious Parenting: Many Paths to Contemplation," Center for Action and Contemplation, June 25, 2019, https://cac.org/daily-meditations/many-paths-to-contemplation-2019-06-25/.

2. Thomas Keating, *Intimacy with God* (New York: Crossroads, 1994), 55.

3. Howard Thurman, "How Good It Is to Center Down," in *Meditations of the Heart* (Boston: Beacon Press, 1981), 28.

4. Joan Chittister, *Illuminated Life: Monastic Wisdom for Seekers of Light* (Maryknoll, NY: Orbis Books, 2000), 70.

smoke, or dance. News to me, since my mother—who was raised a Baptist—did all three.

When I asked my father, "What's the big deal about which religion that I am?" he said that the way that he thought about it was that all over the world, for centuries, people have been worshiping something greater than themselves. To him, that was evidence that there is a God. He invited me to pay more attention to the evidence of the existence of a Divine, Supreme Being than how others chose to worship in an organized way. He also asked me to Love everyone, to pray for peace, and to work to build a community of faith.

In his own way, my father helped me to understand that there are multiple voices—not a single voice—that must be sung together. I do not spend a lot of time thinking about what I am able to do or not do as a Christian African American woman, nor how the "church" has prevented women and African Americans historically from being in leadership roles. Having grown up during the civil rights movement, the freedom song "We Shall Overcome" was both my lullaby and commitment to victory. Armed with graduate degrees from prestigious institutions, I climbed the corporate ranks to become a managing director on Wall Street before retiring. My climb was undergirded by my faith, instilled in me by my parents at an early age.

My father was an AME minister and my mother was raised Baptist. Music was an important way that we experienced centering down. In Daddy's church, no hymnals nor sheet music were on display; the choir and parishioners followed the choir director seamlessly in the call and response. All that was required was a piano and an organ, and maybe a tambourine. We intuitively knew how to clap on the 2 and 4 or to do the double-single hand clap, sometimes even clapping between beats. The organist seemed to know when to speed up playing, as people jumped into the aisles and began to dance, filled with the Holy Spirit.

I remember asking Daddy why some people seemed to get "happy" in church (that's what we called it), waving their hands in the air, shouting and crying, sometimes falling out, clearly overcome with emotion. Church fans made of hard stock paper with a wooden handle provided by the local funeral parlor (with a family pictured on the front of the fan, all decked out in their Sunday best seated in a pew) were used to cool down the parishioners who were stretched out in the aisles. A large, white, freshly pressed cloth was thrown over the legs of the women to preserve modesty while hats and pocketbooks—and even wigs—were safely retrieved.

My father patiently explained that not everybody shouts and dances. His mother, Grandma Matthews, would just stay seated, taking her cane and pounding it on the floor, eyes closed, tears streaming down her cheeks. My father said, "Sometimes life is so hard during the week that the only release is in church on Sunday where they can be one with God." In my mind, they were all finding their respective pathways to centering down and I was witnessing a contemplative experience.

As an African American, I draw upon my own worship experience to find ways to center down. It may mean taking walks while listening to soothing music, journaling, long bike rides as I commune with nature, silent retreats, wisdom circles, prayer vigils, or contemplative prayer. Today, I am a faithful Episcopalian (part of the worldwide Anglican communion) and I consider myself to be what one might think of as a nontraditional contemplative. For on occasion, I've been known to slip into a Black church of any denomination on a Sunday morning to get my gospel fix, closing my eyes as I sway in the pew, raising my right hand, mouthing the refrain, interspersed with a whispered, "Yes, Lord." It is in those moments that I especially feel that I am being still and feeling God's loving presence.

Perhaps it is because, as an African American woman, I have experienced and witnessed so many "isms" in the world. As much as we would like to hope that the "isms" no longer exist—racism, sexism, religionism, ageism, homophobia-ism, disability-ism—they do sadly and disappointingly still do. But through it all, I have never lost hope nor lost my faith.

As the inspirational theologian and writer Barbara Crafton reminds us: Faith is not an amulet, "a magic something you carry around with you to protect you from harm." But faith does help us to discern what Crafton describes as the measures of "bane and blessing" that come our way.[5]

Faith is what lives in you no matter what harm befalls you. It is the assurance of a presence of a higher power (whom I choose to call God ... you may call it Allah, or the Buddha, or Jehovah, or Prophet Mohammed, or Spirit, or the Divine Goddess; whatever you choose to call your higher power, you have the assurance of a presence through the worst and the best of it all).

And while there still may be unanswered questions about what is lost and what is gained in racial and social justice movements within faith traditions, I spend more of my time worshiping the God of Abraham, Jacob, Sarah, Rebekah, and Mary. Yes, the history of an African American Christian is not just his story or just her story—it is your story, and your story, and our story.

Releasing, centering down, becoming one with God. The thirteenth-century poet Rumi wrote: "Let the beauty we love be what we do. There are hundreds of ways to kneel and kiss the ground."[6]

In our increasingly diverse world, there are hundreds—if not thousands—of ways to be a contemplative. Let us open our hearts to make a place for this rich diversity of experiencing stillness ... which may or may not include silence ... as we seek to become

---

5. Barbara Crafton, "Faith Is Not An Amulet/Flee," The Geranium Farm, June 16, 2005. http://geraniumfarm.org/dailyemo.cfm?Emo=503.

6. Jalal al-Din Rumi with Coleman Barks and John Moyne, trans., *Essential Rumi* (San Francisco: HarperOne, 1995), 36.

a welcoming Beloved Community where all can feel a sense of belonging.

Portions of this essay first appeared as "Stillness and Silence as An African American Contemplative" in Shalem Institute Friday Blog (September 16, 2022). Used with permission.

10

---◄►---

Seeing with the Eyes of the Heart

Social Justice and the Art of Spiritual Guidance

Phillip Stephens

n the winter of 2021, the height of the Covid-19 pandemic, I found myself in the middle of yet another Shalem Zoom meeting. The meeting was designed to build community so that our corporate ministry might be more impactful. Thus, there were many plenary sessions followed by small group and paired sharing. During one of the one-to-one sessions, my partner, upon finding out that I had been recently named the program director for Shalem's Spiritual Guidance program, asked, "What does the ministry of spiritual guidance have to do with social justice?" I was surprised by the question because the connection between spiritual guidance and social justice seemed obvious to me. I could tell by the question, however, that it was far from obvious to the one asking.

So, there we were with only fifteen minutes allotted for the entire one-to-one conversation, and we were both to share about our respected ministries. Given the time constraints, I kept my answer short. I responded, "Spiritual guidance has everything to do with social justice, because in the power of the Spirit, the world is literally changed through this ministry."

Truth be told, I was somewhat shocked with my response. I'd never articulated this awareness quite so succinctly before. I was left with a sense that there was much more to my response than I could know and articulate in the moment. Thus, I experienced an invitation to dive into prayer around my conversation partner's question to articulate more fully what I knew in my heart. The following reflections are the fruit of my prayer, and I share them so that other spiritual guides and pilgrims might join me in exploring the significance of their ministry of spiritual guidance in nurturing social justice.

Right up front, I share the prayer with which I center down when preparing for and entering into a spiritual guidance session:

My heart to your heart,
Your heart to mine,
Our hearts indwelling,
May the Lotus bloom.

This prayer always reminds me of Esther Meek's definition of "knowing":

Knowing is the responsible human struggle
to rely on clues
to focus upon a coherent pattern
and submit to its reality.[1]

Meek's reflections invite us to experience knowing as an ongoing process of discernment rather than an accomplished feat. It seems to me that when we embrace knowing as a process, it is inherently nondual because new clues are always arising. This understanding

---

1. Esther Lightcap Meek, *Longing to Know: The Philosophy of Knowledge for Ordinary People* (Grand Rapids, MI: Brazos Press, 2003), 13.

is profoundly contemplative. Gabriel Marcel expresses it so well: "Contemplation is the practice of attending wholly to God."[2] What does all this have to do with the ministry of spiritual guidance? I understand spiritual guidance to be a ministry of prayer involving the Holy Spirit, a spiritual pilgrim, and a spiritual companion. The pilgrim, within this corporate prayer, seeks to discern the Holy Spirit's invitations for a spiritual journey. As the Holy Spirit is the actual guide within this prayerful encounter, the discernment of the Spirit's invitations involves "a first-person form of knowing that possesses intimacy and directness, as it is both based on and the fruit of *here and now awareness* of one's unveiled experience of reality, which includes a direct and non-conceptual experience of one's own existence."[3] This pilgrimage of discernment is a grace-filled voyage of discovery characterized by welcoming mystery, loving encounter, pledging transformation, inviting dance, and indwelling Shalom. Both the pilgrim and companion are often invited to journey to foreign places they never imagined visiting.

A session with a pilgrim from a number of years ago comes to mind. In this session, the pilgrim and I were invited to explore issues of social justice within her spiritual journey. After a busy morning on a brilliant spring day—one of those cool, crisp days pulsing with energy—I put away everything, said Noonday Prayer, and sat quietly in the Presence awaiting the pilgrim's arrival. When she arrived, we greeted one another, lit a candle, and sat for a few minutes in silence. Then, she began to share vignettes from her spiritual journey, experiences of one devoted to social justice ministry for the imprisoned, sick, poor, and hungry.

As the pilgrim shared her concerns, I became aware she seemed to be expressing a deep-seated anger toward the powers,

---

2. David J. Kettle, *Western Culture in Gospel Context: Towards the Conversion of the West: Theological Bearings for Mission and Spirituality* (Eugene, OR: Cascade Books, 2011), 33.

3. Han F. de Wit, *Contemplative Psychology*, trans. Marie Louise Baird (Pittsburgh: Duquesne University Press, 1987), 33.

principalities, and individuals whom she considered responsible for the plight of those she served. Although I sensed a nudge to ask a question, another part of me said, "Wait." Thus, I continued to listen as I felt the Spirit drawing us more fully into the Presence—a movement through the depths of our being as we were mutually enfolded within the Spirit's embrace. We were plunged into the silent depths of an obscure, pregnant womb where we shared the pilgrim's concerns from the common altar of our hearts with no verbal communication.

This silent womb was not what might readily spring to mind when thinking of silence. It was anything but quiet. As the pilgrim and I sat together, the sounds of the world exploded around us. Birds sang; carpenters hammered; and appliances started and stopped. It was the ultimate *musique concrète*—the Spirit playing creation's symphony through us. Life-giving energy enfolded and penetrated us, uniting our hearts with the heartbeat of creation. We were acutely present—calmed and energized at the same time.

As the silence dissipated, it felt like emerging from an invigorating swim. We rested in the glow. The unasked question nudged its way again into consciousness. Finally, I shared, "I wonder what feelings are coming up for you." She responded, "I'm really angry." Then I asked, 'How is your anger life-giving?'" The pilgrim pondered the question silently for some time before responding. "It's not—not for me, not for those I serve, and not for those I blame." I asked, "How are you sharing your anger with God?" She quickly responded, "I'm not." Then I wondered aloud, "How might it be if you were to intentionally pray for all these folks—friend and foe?" After another extended silence, she observed, "Although the world's externals might not change, my relationship with them might be different." After another silence, she shared that she had been willfully holding onto her anger, but during our shared silence had begun to sense that the energy may not be hers to hold.

She said, "I'm feeling a need to release all these people into God's hands." She wondered, "Could it be that God's inviting me to open my heart to the Grace of the moment? You know, let go and let God show me how to be present in a life-giving way with both those I serve and those I blame?"

My reflections upon the above session proceed from an understanding of actively engaging in social justice through the lens of the Christian gospel as recorded in the Summary of the Law. It places the call to love and witness right at the heart of the Christian vocation:

> "You shall love the Lord your God with all your heart and with all your soul and with all your mind." This is the greatest and first commandment. And a second is like it: "You shall love your neighbor as yourself." On these two commandments hang all the law and the prophets.[4]

It seems to me that in this passage, Jesus unites the Sh'ma and the Golden Rule with the phrase "*and a second is like it.*" He teaches through this union that we love God with our entire being when we love our neighbors as ourselves. Elizabeth O'Connor states it bluntly:

> That is what Christianity is all about—becoming lovers. The mission of the church is just loving people. And our confession? What is our confession? It is that we do not know how to love. Until we have made that confession, there is nothing to be learned. We cannot even be a beginner with the beginners, and in the School of Christianity there is nothing else to be but a beginner.[5]

Thus, as the Summary of the Law is incarnate within our lives, we become lovers who understand everyone deserves equal economic, political and social rights and opportunities. And we are called to

---

4. Matthew 22:37–40 (NRSV)
5. Elizabeth O'Connor, *Search for Silence* (Waco, TX: Word Books, 1972), 21.

open the doors of access and opportunity for everyone, particularly those in greatest need."

The refrain from one of my favorite hymns emerges into consciousness, "Where charity and love dwell, God himself is there."[6] It comes to mind because I sense in the above session a manifestation of the inherently social exchange of freely affirming energy known as "love." Pondering the session, I marvel at how the Spirit drew the pilgrim and me into the depths of the Presence where we communed from the heart to the point of mutual transcendence. The communion looked and felt like *agape*, the love that flows from the heart of God through the Incarnation into our space/time continuum. "The Word became flesh and lived among us, and we have seen his glory."[7] It is the transfiguring and all-transforming love of Christ that obliges us to leave the security of our various states of certitude that are often forms of bondage and launch out into the wilderness with no clear sense of destination.[8] I am reminded of Mary Ann Donovan's summary of Irenaeus of Lyon's teachings:

> While God remains unknown in greatness, God is always known in love. God is like a loving parent, whose strength and wisdom far exceed the comprehension of an infant, but who yet speaks tender words of love to that infant. Indeed, as the baby comes forth from its mother, so the world, in its very beginnings, came directly from the hands of the creator. The one God, the Father, used God's hands, the Word and the Wisdom (the Son and the Spirit), to create, to shape, and to adorn all things. . . . So too, God shaped the first human; it was God-and no lesser being-who breathed the breath of life into the face of that first human being and imprinted the divine image in its very flesh. . . .

---

6. *Ubi caritas*, plainsong, MODE 8, from *The Hymnal 1982* (New York: The Church Pension Fund, 1985), 606. Trans. Phillip Stephens.

7. John 1:14 (NRSV)

8. Frank T. Griswold. "Text of Presiding Bishop Griswold's Friday Sermon from General Convention of the Episcopal Church: Reiterating Themes of Receive, Repent, Reconcile, Restore" (New York: Episcopal News Service, 2003).

Far from being remote, God is immediate to us in our very materiality.[9]

I wonder, "What is the significance, within spiritual guidance, of God being immediate to us in our very materiality?" Could it be that we encounter God in the very being of every person we encounter— friend and stranger, ally and perceived foe, including self? My experience of the Christian tradition leads me to respond, "Yes!"

> By the love the Holy Spirit pours into Christian hearts at baptism we are empowered to grow in the faith that works through love until we spontaneously see God in his images, our neighbors and ourselves. This we do with the eyes of the heart, the heart standing for the human person as a unity of mind, will and affection.[10]

The Hindu greeting *Namaste* gives voice to this Divine encounter. Namaste: That which is Divine within me honors that which is Divine within you. God is immediate to us through our very materiality. We are all miraculous manifestations of God's love.

As I consider the lives of those within the Christian tradition who seem to exemplify Namaste, I am drawn to the prototypes for contemplative spiritual guidance, the Desert Mothers and Fathers. Within the depths of their being, they pledged themselves to God's transforming love through an encounter with one another. They were not big on talking, but they were big on loving communion. When they opened their hearts to God for the other in spiritual guidance, the other appears to have been a primary source of the Word of God within the encounter. The famous story of Abba Lot and Abba Joseph comes to mind:

---

9. Mary Ann Donovan, "Irenaeus: At the Heart of Life, Glory," in *Spiritualties of the Heart: Approaches to Personal Wholeness in Christian Tradition*, ed. Annice Callahan (Mahwah, NJ: Paulist Press, 1990), 12.

10. Mary T. Clark, "Augustine: The Eye of the Heart," in Callahan, *Spiritualties of the Heart*, 31.

> Abba Lot went to see Abba Joseph and said to him, "Abba, as far as I can I say my little office, I fast a little, I pray and meditate, I live in peace and as far as I can, I purify my thoughts. What else can I do?" Then the old man stood up and stretched his hands towards heaven. His fingers became like ten lamps of fire and he said to him, "If you will, you can become all flame."[11]

Within the encounter, Joseph hears the voice of God calling from the depths of Lot's heart expressing a desire to become more perceptibly incarnate. Experiencing the voice of God through Lot, Joseph allows his own heart, ignited by God's love, to burst into flame. Only then does he dare speak, fanning the spark within his companion.

There seems to be a parallel between the story of the Abbas and the session with my pilgrim. As the Spirit moved to open my heart to the Presence with the pilgrim, I seemed to hear its faint voice calling from the depths of the pilgrim's heart. It seemed to express a desire for a more intimate relationship with the Ground of Being, *in all being*; i.e., the pilgrim's desire to find a way to nurture her relationship with God while honoring both those she served *and* those whose actions challenged her worldview. As I listened for the Spirit's movement within our intimate dance, the Spirit nudged my heart to stand with the pilgrim's need in the midst of the Holy Mystery we call God—not with an intent to solve a problem or find an answer, but to share invitations and wonderings for the pilgrim's journey as revealed through our encounter. The pilgrim, in turn, was called through her story to stand silently with me in the midst of the Divine Mystery. We were invited by the Spirit into the mysterious dance of *intercession* (from the Latin, "inter" plus "cedere," meaning "to stand among or between"). St. Paul's wonderful hymn of incarnate love comes to mind:

---

11. Benedicta Ward, *The Sayings of the Desert Fathers: The Alphabetical Collection* (Kalamazoo, MI: Cistercian Publications, 1975), 103.

[T]hough ... in the form of God, [Christ Jesus] did not regard equality with God as something to be exploited, but emptied himself, taking the form of a slave, being born in human likeness. And being found in human form, he humbled himself and became obedient to the point of death—even death on a cross. Therefore, God also highly exalted him and gave him the name that is above every name.[12]

As the pilgrim and I were drawn through intercession into the *Prayer of Presence,* a deep opening to experiencing all being simultaneously, we experienced a glimpse of heaven—the healing of the ages. The pilgrim was reminded that the Ground of Being, through the power of the Spirit, sustains her within our space/time continuum and that she need seek no further than her own heart in relation to another to experience the loving intimacy of God's embrace. She was invited to observe the dance between willingness and willfulness fueled by her anger:

Willingness implies a surrendering of one's self-separateness, an entering-into, an immersion in the deepest processes of life itself. ... More simply, willingness is saying yes to the mystery of being alive in each moment. Willfulness is saying no, or perhaps more commonly, "Yes, but ..." Sooner or later a choice will have to be made: to continue on a willful ... path in which one tries to secure autonomy and self-determination, or to embark on a spiritual path in which one seeks ever-greater willingness to become a part of the fundamental processes of life in self-surrender.[13]

During our session, the pilgrim was enabled, by grace, to step through her anger and embark on a spiritual path in which she sought an ever-greater willingness to become a part of the fundamental processes of life. Subsequently, over the years, I have

---

12. Philippians 2:6–9 (NRSV)
13. Gerald G. May, *Will and Spirit: A Contemplative Psychology* (San Francisco: Harper, 1982), 6, 27.

witnessed how her grace-filled step has transformed her social justice ministry. Her commitment to securing equal economic, political, and social opportunity for everyone grows stronger every day. Yet, her ministry is more effective than ever because she is able to perceive, honor, name, and trust the transforming Light of Christ within the powers, principalities, and individuals whom she considers responsible for the plight of those she serves.

As the companion within this relationship, I was invited to experience spiritual guidance as a marriage of the conceptual systems of the Western tradition with the non-conceptual gifts of the Ground of Being as incarnated and experienced *through all being*—a marriage characterized by welcoming mystery, loving encounter, pledging transformation, inviting dance, and indwelling Shalom. Honoring the covenant of this marriage, I was invited to step respectfully through the icons of methods and techniques of the conceptual realm into the experience of Divine Mystery and respond through the spirit to God *with the pilgrim*. As James Otis Sargent Huntington observed, "Love must act as light must shine and fire must burn," a phenomenal awareness from which to engage the ministries of social justice and spiritual guidance.[14]

Also, being a companion on my pilgrim's journey over the years, I have witnessed how sitting with a pilgrim can literally change the world. I have also come to understand that the potential observable characteristics of any guidance relationship are myriad given the uniqueness of each pilgrim with whom I journey coupled with the variable circumstances of any given day. Thus, embracing this grace-filled pilgrimage, I am continually invited to trust in the assurance of the Spirit's desire to transform my human frailties into opportunities for the outpouring of God's infinite, life-giving *Love*.

---

14. Order of the Holy Cross, *The Rule of James Otis Sargent Huntington and His Successors* (West Park, NY: Holy Cross Publications, 1991), 15.

11

Coming to Our Senses
Embracing Wonder and Gratitude
Leah Moran Rampy

"To be alive in this beautiful, self-organizing universe—to participate in the dance of life with senses to perceive it, lungs that breathe it, organs that draw nourishment from it—it is a wonder beyond words."[1]
—Joanna Macy

"The Divine communicates to us primarily through the language of the natural world. Not to hear the natural world is not to hear the Divine."[2]
—Thomas Berry

Why take time in our busy lives to slow our pace, to allow the space to receive awe and wonder? A recent study found that a sense of wonder promotes loving-kindness and altruism, helps reduce inflammation, and improves our immune system. No wonder (pun intended!) so many people found solace outdoors during the recent pandemic. In the UK, some hospitals experimented with "secret gardens," wheeling intensive care patients into the sunshine on a patio surrounded by blooming potted plants.

---

1. Joanna Macy, "Work That Reconnects; Personal Guidelines," n.d., September 5, 2022. https://workthatreconnects.org/spiral/the-great-turning/personal-guidelines/.
2. Thomas Berry, *The Sacred Universe: Earth, Spirituality, and Religion in the Twenty-First Century*, ed. Mary Evelyn Tucker (New York: Columbia University Press, 2009).

The personal testimonies of very ill individuals who came back to themselves in the sunlight are touching and powerful.[3]

A field of research and preventative care in Japan, *shinrin-yoku*, or forest bathing, invites one to several hours of slow wandering among trees.[4] This connection to the woods can decrease stress and engender a greater sense of well-being. The Kaiser-Permanente website gives a nod to forest bathing and recommends "awe walks" for one's health.[5] It does seem that being outdoors, open to wonder, can aid our well-being.

But I can't help thinking that it's a very lopsided relationship if we focus only on the benefits to ourselves! Such self-absorption would not serve a friendship, a marriage, or a soul connection. Instead of walking in the woods for our personal benefit alone, what if we opened ourselves to the living beings around us. We might consider listening for their wisdom, becoming curious about their connections, tuning in to their needs, and offering appreciation for their gifts to the world.

And what about listening for the ever-present Sacred One who enlivens our soul? Many of us find that time attending to the wonder of this amazing cosmos helps to further open our hearts to God. The song of the stars, the call of the wren, the glimmer of a dragonfly, the scent of the pines—all contribute to the holy dance in which we are enveloped. Captured by awe and wonder, we are invited to remember our unbreakable connection to the Sacred Mystery in which everything is held in oneness.

3. Steven Morris, "Back to Nature: 'Secret Garden' Outings Used to Aid Coronavirus Recovery," *The Guardian*, May 5, 2020, sec. World news, https://www.theguardian.com/world/2020/may/05/back-to-nature-secret-garden-outings-used-to-aid-coronavirus-recovery.

4. "Shinrin-Yoku, "The Simple and Intuitive Form of Preventative Care," *Portland Japanese Garden* (blog), August 15, 2022, https://japanesegarden.org/2022/08/15/shinrin-yoku/.

5. "Forest Bathing: What It Is and Why You Should Try It," Kaiser Permanente, December 19, 2022, https://thrive.kaiserpermanente.org/thrive-together/live-well/forest-bathing-try.

A delight of this life is that beauty, awe, and wonder can capture our attention when we least expect it. We walk along lost in thought and suddenly we are enthralled. The sun painting the sky in reds and golds, cloudscapes of which no artist could dream, soaring majestic blue mountains, streams babbling with joyous abandon, tiny communities embedded in a center of a flower, oaks in a mast year prolific with acorns—wonder can take hold in any moment. Indeed, day after day, moment by moment, nature pours out her gifts, showering us with immense, microscopic, abundant, sparse, vibrant, soft offerings—all freely given. Sadly, we do not always receive the gift of wonder, even when it is right before us. Earth offers herself, and we hurry on past with eyes focused on our list of things to do.

One of the reasons that I have loved the opportunity to lead pilgrimages is that participants receive encouragement and space to practice seeing with "pilgrim eyes," a soft gaze that invites opening to awe and wonder. We begin this practice by connecting ourselves to ground below and sky above. Our breath slows, drops, deepens. Our eyes soften, inviting sights to come to us. When *gazing*, we let our eyes rest on what is inviting our awareness without expectation.

When we gaze in that open and unhurried way, we allow for unique expressions of beauty within each member of the kin-dom. We let go of any place else we need to be, of anything else we *must* do. We are more fully *here*, in this place. Our hearts have the space to truly see the more-than-human life around us. Pathways open between us and other beings, and we risk sharing our true selves. We trust that communion, soul to soul with kindred beings, is available in this moment.

Time and again, I have witnessed pilgrims blessed by the beauty of old growth forests on the Olympic Peninsula or the stones that hold centuries of prayer on the Isle of Iona. Off the coast of Newfoundland, our hearts expanded to include puffins, whales, and abundant bird life as kin while they swam, leapt, flew, and relished their place in the family of things. It's in the tiniest of things too: delicate plants at the base of the hemlocks; stones flecked with green marble polished by the sea, ferns peeking through the layers of thirteenth-century stone walls.

A pilgrimage is special because we spend time in places saturated by prayer, set aside distractions to be fully present, remind each other to slow, receive the company of kindred spirits, and are accompanied by leaders who guide gently and prayerfully to a place of ever-deeper awareness. But travel and companionship are not required for this practice. You can bring these same intentions to a walk in your backyard or a nearby park. Moments of wonder can be found by lying on your back to observe the vastness of the night sky, knowing that what you can see—as amazing as it is—is only a fraction of a fraction of stars and galaxies in the vast cosmos. Take a magnifying glass and really look at the rich and beautifully complex landscapes in a dot of moss. Watch the sunsets. Listen to birdsong. Be fully open to the Sacred unity of the life around you, here, now.

There are myriad of ways to open our hearts; being fully present in nature is not the only way, but it is a way. In each moment, we choose whether or not to take this journey. When we slow enough to gaze upon the world, we are almost always greeted with gifts of beauty, awe, and wonder. And as Robin Wall Kimmerer reminded us in her beautiful book *Braiding Sweetgrass*, a gift creates a relationship.[6]

* * *

Here is one practice that may assist you in expanding your awareness of beauty, awe, and connection. Find a place outdoors where you will not be too distracted. Sit, stand, or lie down, whatever is comfortable for you. Ground yourself here, sensing your connection to the earth below and the sky above. Take a few long, deep breaths; then let your breath slow and deepen as it comes to

---

6. Robin Wall Kimmerer, *Braiding Sweetgrass; Indigenous Wisdom, Scientific Knowledge, and the Teachings of Plants* (Minneapolis, MN: Milkweed Editions, 2015), 111.

a normal rhythm. Relax your shoulders, jaw, eyes, and any other places where you are holding tension. Open your heart.

Now attend to your hearing. You might want to close your eyes to focus all your attention on listening. Don't strain to pick up sounds; quiet your thoughts and let them come to you. For five to ten minutes or whatever is right for you, simply stay with listening. When you find that your mind has wandered to something else, gently bring your attention back to what you are hearing. We tend to separate what we hear into sounds of nature, people, and mechanical things. See if you can omit the labels and the judgments that attach themselves to the labels. Let whatever is given in each moment wash over you.

When it seems invited, move on to the next of your sense and repeat. Of course, take care of yourself, especially with tasting, and make sure that you know what is safe for you. You might find it meaningful to focus on your sense of taste as you begin your next meal.

When you have completed this practice, journal about what you noticed. When did you feel most open and connected to the Sacred? What might have gotten in your way of such a connection? What do you want to take with you into the rest of your day? On days when you feel too rushed to complete the full practice, simply deepen your attention with one of your senses.

* * *

As you walk along the forest trail, your footsteps crunching leaves and cracking twigs, you alert the dwellers there to your presence. You may hear rustling and see bushes waving in the wake of a departure. Birds take flight, sharing with others through their movement and calls. Insects change their tune or hush into silence. Trees and plants communicate with each other, sending messages via the underground fungal network as well as through the release of aerosols. Although some of these aerosols rise into the air and blend with water vapor to plant the seeds of rain, others infuse the air around the tree canopy as a welcome or warning signal to other trees.[7]

Decades ago, scientists found that acacia trees in the African savannah immediately pumped toxic substances to their leaves when they felt hungry giraffes beginning to nibble on them. As other trees in the vicinity sensed the gas emitted from the gnawed-upon trees, they too took precautionary measures and added toxin to their leaves. Giraffes had to move away from the area or downwind to get ahead of the trees' early warning network.[8]

Beeches, spruce, and oaks register pain as leaves are eaten by caterpillars and send electrical signals through underground fungal networks to alert other trees. However, if the roots are in trouble, a back-up communication process takes over and the leaves release scent compounds to warn their neighbors of impending danger. Trees can also release pheromones to call for help from specific beneficial insects. Scents emitted from fruit trees, willows, and chestnuts beckon passing bees. What a wonder! Communication through scent is happening all around us! Parenthetically and sadly, our methods of selective breeding for many plants, especially food crops, has eliminated the plants' ability to communicate with their kin. Most industrial farm fields are silent, easy prey for insect pests, thereby "justifying" the application of pesticides, the harm rippling through waterways and bloodstreams.[9]

Imagine all these tiny molecules wafting from tree to tree throughout the forest. You breathe them into your lungs as you walk in these woods, the microbiome of your body meeting the molecules born of the trees. Imagine how these signals may differ in a plant community under threat and one where individuals are

---

7. Diana Beresford-Kroeger, *To Speak for the Trees: My Life's Journey from Ancient Celtic Wisdom to a Healing Vision of the Forest* (Toronto: Random House Canada, 2019), 168.

8. Peter Wohlleven, *The Hidden Language of Trees: What They Feel, How They Communicate*, trans. Jane Billinghurst (Berkeley, CA: Greystone Books, 2015), 7.

9. Wohlleven, *Hidden Language of Trees*, 7–12.

safe. Does wandering within a recently harvested or newly planted woodland feel the same to you as walking in an old growth forest? Studies have shown that blood pressure is lowered in stands of old oaks.[10] No wonder ancient oaks have been considered sacred by untold generations of peoples!

As you walk along the forest trail, attend to each breath. What are you taking in? Do you sense any way in which the trees may be communing with you? What might they notice as you breath out? When your heart fills with love and gratitude, is that message carried on the molecules you release to the forest community? Are aerosols of your indifference or anger transmitted to the trees? When the mother tree tells others of your presence, is it a warning or a welcome? Are the trees thankful for you?

Every single breath. The water we drink. Food. Shelter. Sun, shade, climate that permits life. Earth regularly showers us with gifts of wonder and sustenance! Too often we take for granted what is most abundant—and what we most urgently need for life itself. Practices of giving thanks are at the heart of all major spiritual traditions, arguably none more eloquent and expansive than that of the Thanksgiving Address of the Haudenosaunee Confederacy Known in the Onondaga language as the "Words That Come Before All Else,"[11] this practice acknowledges the many gifts of the natural world and offers thanks to the kin who gift us with all that is needed for life. Individually acknowledging each of these many gifts reminds us that we are wealthy indeed.

Many years ago, the journal *Nature* coined the term "wood wide web" to explain scientist Suzanne Simard's work on how trees communicate among themselves through the underground fungal network. In one early study, Simard found that birch and fir trees shared sunshine and nutrients, each taking the lead in supporting

---

10. Wohlleven, *Hidden Language of Trees*, 223.
11. Kimmerer, *Braiding Sweetgrass*, 111.

the other in the season most favorable to their growth. These trees lived in an ongoing exchange of giving and receiving. Reciprocity.

Robin Wall Kimmerer writes of the pure gifts that arise from plants such as the serviceberry. A serviceberry requires no payment or proof of worthiness in exchange for food and medicine for humans, pollen for insects, and food for butterfly larvae, birds, moose, and deer. When we take the time to attend to amazing gifts so freely given, our response is often a welling of gratitude. From such a sense of generous abundance comes a desire to give back, to offer our own gifts in return as thanks. There are many ways to give back: a bow, a song, a poem, a drink of water, a commitment to protect.

Gratitude and reciprocity "have the remarkable property of multiplying with every exchange," wrote Kimmerer.[12] Unlike with *products or money,* relationships between giver and receiver are established with *gifts.* You feel thankful—and responsible. In this way, gifts increase in value as they move from one individual to another. And Earth is always giving. You might say that acknowledging gifts, responding in gratitude, and returning gifts in reciprocity is a well-established Earth practice.

Yet, the concept of exchanging gifts with the natural world may feel countercultural to us. In the United States our laws reinforce the idea of land *belonging* to us to *use for our personal benefit.* With a few notable exceptions, non–human beings have no rights—to our shame, that is true for some humans as well. We speak of *natural resources* and the language implies that they are ours for the taking. Notice the world of difference in the attitude and impact of *consuming resources* and *receiving gifts.* Which contributes to a sense of joy and well-being? Which practice nurtures us in our grief? Feeds our souls? If we were to embrace living in a world of gifts, how might it change us and our relationship with others? With all beings in the web of life?

---

12. Robin Wall Kimmerer, "The Serviceberry: An Economy of Abundance," *Emergence Magazine,* October 26, 2022, https://emergencemagazine.org/essay/the-serviceberry/. September 5, 2022.

Benedictine monk Brother David Steindl-Rast has written for many years about gratitude as a pathway to joy and fulfillment. Teacher and cofounder of Gratefulness.org, his wisdom is a balm for the soul. He affirms that the commitment we make to live in communion with and gratitude for this world: "A lifetime may not be long enough to attune ourselves fully to the harmony of the universe. But just to become aware that we can resonate with it—that alone can be like waking up from a dream."[13]

With such an abundance of life-giving gifts, why are we not living in a permanent state of gratitude? At least in part, we have become habituated to seeing with the eyes of our mind. Our minds love to stay busy planning and organizing the future or replaying the past. When we see primarily with the eyes of the mind, we find it difficult to fully *experience* the present moment. And it is in the present moment that we open to awe and wonder; succumb to love and compassion; feel joy, grief, and gratitude; and experience the presence of the Holy One. When we shift to seeing with the eyes of our heart, we can more fully experience a long, loving look at the real. From that contemplative space, we increase our capacity for deeper relationships with others and with Earth.

Seeing with the eyes of the heart can be an intentional practice. We can make a conscious choice to drop our attention into our heart space, slowing to expand our capacity for awareness. Then the seeds of gratitude are planted. We can choose to direct our attention to those seeds, nurture them, and make the space for gratitude to grow. This way of being is a gift of grace.

At some point, you may have been encouraged to keep a gratitude journal—and perhaps you are engaged in this practice now. Research has found that keeping a gratitude journal reduces stress, supports psychological health, increases empathy and reduces

---

13. Brother David Steindl-Rast, *Words of Common Sense for Mind, Body and Soul* (West Conshohocken, PA: Templeton Press, 2002), 10.

aggression, results in healthier relationships, improves sleep, increases self-esteem, makes for a longer and happier life ... the list actually goes on![14] Surely this list is sufficient to understand that attending to gratitude benefits you personally. And what of the benefits to Earth and the beings whose lives we hold in our hands in a multitude of decisions we make daily?

Loving relationships within human families are enhanced by feelings of gratitude. Is it any surprise that getting in touch with our gratitude for the more-than-human beings who nurture our bodies, lift our spirits, and feed our souls enhances our loving relationships with them? Our souls thrive in deep communion within the cosmic family. We can demonstrate our love for the world through our relationships with specific soul places and beings. We can expand our loving relationship moment by moment: in *this* pause to absorb the beauty, *this* heartfelt expression of gratitude, *this* offering of gifts to our beloved. We can choose to repeat this time and again until our souls find their home in the endlessly flowing exchange of gratitude and love.

* * *

We kick off wet hiking shoes, don the requisite soft-soled slippers, and struggle up the wide stone steps to stand at last on the tilted slab of sandstone and mudstone that hangs over the water's edge. We have driven through the misty morning to the southeastern tip of Newfoundland's Avalon Peninsula to visit Mistaken Point Ecological Reserve to see for ourselves possible sites for a future Shalem pilgrimage.

I imagine a relatively easy guided walk from our cars to the water's edge, but the usual way is closed due to flooding. Instead, we are led

14. "Science Explains 12 Benefits of Keeping a Gratitude Journal," Power of Positivity, November 11, 2019, accessed August 30, 2022, https://www.powerofpositivity.com/science-explains-12-benefits-gratitude-journal/.

on a trek across rain-saturated bogland, our guide setting a pace that, along with the uneven footing, tests my endurance. There is nothing on the horizon; we are alone in the vastness. Wait! In the distance a small herd of caribou appear and are stopped silently in their tracks by our approach. Perhaps I might be excused from trekking further to watch these large mammals I have never seen before. I look for a bench, a stump, or even a rock where I could sit until the guide collects me on the return trip. Nothing. All is soggy bog. Beauty lies in the smallest of mosses and occasional wildflowers with dime-sized blossoms, but our group is instructed to stay together, and we do not pause.

At last, to my relief, we reach our destination. Yellow wildflowers grace the cliff edge and waves beat against the rocky shoreline below as the sea summons her energy from beyond the fog. Yet our collective attention is not fixed on this beautiful ocean scene, for we are standing in soft slippers on fossils of the oldest, largest, most complex life-forms found anywhere on Earth. A generous smattering of some of the 10,000 fossils from a prehistoric sea are captured in stone at our feet. Known to scientists as the Ediacara biota, these species began some 580 million years ago when all life was in the sea. They survived there for millions of years.[15]

Arrayed at our feet is a testament to life from time beyond our imagining. Mud and sandstone have preserved this story of an ocean floor community and held it fast through 565 million years of evolution. Here on this fog-enveloped oceanside, we walk with the fossils, sit beside them, try to glimpse the immensity of what we are seeing. We humans are such a tiny blip in Earth's lifespan!

The trek back to our car is just as long, just as wet, boggy, and uneven, just as difficult for my always-troublesome knee. But my spiritual heart has invited my mind to a conversation about more than my physical comfort. What is our place in this family of things

---

15. "Mistaken Point Ecological Reserve and UNESCO World Heritage Site," Department of Environment and Climate Change, accessed September 1, 2022, https://www.gov .nl.ca/ecc/natural-areas/wer/r-mpe/.

from time-we-cannot-imagine? Who are we all in this kin-dom of beings, cycling through birth and death, evolution and extinction? How can I possibly hold in my mind these miracles of creation? I have no answers. Still, I am grateful to be nudged out of the small details of daily life to wonder at the immensity of deep time and consider our place in the ongoing evolution of life on Earth.

It's been four years since the walk to Mistaken Point and the opportunity to sit with that ancient story. The group of pilgrims for which we prepared has come and gone. I've since taken a class to better understand the great extinction events that have occurred throughout Earth's history. My husband and I created a cosmic walk,[16] scaling down the 13.8 billion years since the great flaring forth into a walkable timeline of the universe. I've written about Earth's evolution to highlight the barely-a-blink time in which humans have walked this land. Despite those efforts, I am no closer to understanding the larger questions I pondered on that wet walk back from the fossils. How fortunate that a state of wonder does not require knowledge, only the presence to receive the gifts in each moment. That is more than enough.

I once heard poet Scott Russell Sanders say that we need moments when our self dissolves, and we realize that our sense of separateness is an illusion. Ahh! That's the miracle of awe and wonder: our "little self" fades and our soul is freed to acknowledge her oneness within the vastness of the ever-present Spirit. Taken by awe and wonder, we disappear into the seeing. We become aware of who we have always been, a child of Earth, held in the Holy.

16. Miriam MacGillis and Rhonda Fabian, "An Interview with Sister Miriam Therese MacGillis at Genesis Farm," *Kosmos Journal* (blog), accessed September 17, 2022, https://www.kosmosjournal.org/article/an-interview-with-sister-miriam-therese-macgillis-at-genesis-farm/.

12

Embodying Contemplative Leadership

Howard Thurman and Feeding the Timeless Hunger of the Human Spirit

Lerita Coleman Brown

Introduction

Recently, near the end of a retreat I was leading, a gentleman raised his hand and commented, "I cannot believe Howard Thurman possessed such wisdom. If I saw him on the street, I would have just seen a black man walking. I cannot believe how much I've missed throughout my life." This apt disclosure stirred me to ponder if I or anyone can identify a contemplative or contemplative leader. Do they dress or speak in a unique manner or come from specific faith traditions? Do contemplatives display particular characteristics? How is a contemplative leader different from other leaders? How are they nourished and how do their lives nurture others? My mind rippled with many questions. The answers to some I found in the life and teachings of the great mystic, theologian, modern-day shaman, sacred activist, and contemplative leader, Howard Washington Thurman (1899–1981). For me, Thurman remains a prototype for contemplative living and leadership.

Growing up I was unfamiliar with the term "contemplative," despite my Catholic school attendance. As a young girl, I loved sitting outside in the wind and basking in its gentle serenity. As I grew older, I observed nature with delight; the changing seasons, mountain vistas, roaring oceans, pollinating bees, butterflies, and hummingbirds, and hawks gliding across the sky. Sometimes I would run inside to share my wonder, my sense of feeling like the sun, the moon, and the trees all at once. Yet I didn't have a vocabulary to name these activities or to associate them or myself with a contemplative life.

Initially, I thought a contemplative prayed and meditated all day and resided in a cloistered religious community. I possessed this image of contemplative living for most of my adult life. After being directed to the life and work of Howard Thurman, I uncovered a role model who lived and worked among everyday people and modeled contemplative living.

Howard Thurman is better known in select seminaries and at some Historically Black Colleges and Universities (HBCUs). But details about him and his spiritual contributions have not been widely disseminated outside of limited academic and theological circles. As the demand for lectures and retreats about him increases, I realize his living wisdom still feeds the spiritual thirst and hunger of spiritual seekers some forty years after his death.

His life, writings, sermons, and public lectures are filled with gems of wisdom about the power of silence, nature, self-reflection, and introspection. His call to seek the Presence of God in all things and to spark that sense of Presence in others changed the course of American history. What attributes did he possess that might characterize him as a contemplative leader and highlight the gifts of contemplative living? Strolling through the ways Thurman sought the Presence; championed silence, stillness, and solitude; lived as a holy child of God; cultivated a curious scrutiny; modeled a prophetic spirituality and sacred activism; and walked with inner authority provide us with touchstones of contemplative living and leadership.

Seeks the Presence

A perusal of *With Head and Heart: The Autobiography of Howard Thurman* suggests that he was born a contemplative. Instead of succumbing to the horrors of life in the Jim Crow South in the early 1900s, Howard Thurman felt compelled to turn inside to God. In his book *Footprints of a Dream: The Story of the Church for the Fellowship of All Peoples*, Thurman describes how he experienced a deep, inviting Presence that he didn't experience any other place—not even in church:

> I was a very sensitive child who suffered much from the violences of racial conflict. The climate of our town, Daytona Beach, Florida, was better than most Southern towns because of the influence of the tourists who wintered there. Nevertheless, life became more and more suffocating because of the fear of being brutalized, beaten, or otherwise outraged. In my effort to keep this fear from corroding my life and making me seek relief in shiftlessness, I sought help from God. I found that the more I turned to prayer, to what I discovered in later years to be meditation, the more time I spent alone in the woods or on the beach, the freer became my own spirit and the more realistic became my ambitions to get an education.[1]

It is unclear whether Thurman felt drawn to the peaceful silence outdoors or sought nature's stillness to assuage his terror. His contemplative life expanded beyond sitting to include transcendent moments and his sense of a connection to all.

> As a boy in Florida, I [Thurman] walked along the beach of the Atlantic in the quiet stillness that can only be completely felt when the murmur of the ocean is stilled and the tides move stealthily along the shore. I held my breath against the night and

---

1. Howard Thurman, *Footprints of a Dream: The Story of the Church for the Fellowship of All Peoples* (Eugene, OR: Wipf & Stock, 2009), 16.

watched the stars etch their brightness on the face of the darkened canopy of the heavens. I had the sense that all things, the sand, the sea, the stars, the night, and I were one lung through which all of life breathed. Not only was I aware of a vast rhythm enveloping all, but I was a part of it and it was a part of me.[2]

Thurman held a unique relationship with nature, both basking in the Presence of God and relating aspects of it to life lessons. One of his closest companions as a boy was a large old oak tree in his backyard. When he sat against it, he felt "the same peace that would come to [him] in [his] bed at night;" he shared his "bruises" and his "joys" with the oak and knew that he was "understood."[3]

His intrigue with nature included animals, particularly Emperor Penguins. He wrote, "The signature of God is all around me, in the rocks, in the trees, in the minds of [men]."[4] He used his observations about the deep rootedness of plants during winter, storms emerging from the ocean, and dazzlingly sunsets to aid him and others in their spiritual growth. These early experiences influenced Thurman's entire approach to life, spirituality, religion, and his relationship with God. They also allowed him to realize his full potential despite the exigencies of racial discrimination and the demonization of black men.

Champions Silence
and Other Contemplative Activities

Howard Thurman realized from an early age that there was something special about a contemplative atmosphere. Often when we think of contemplative, we immediately imagine ourselves isolated and sitting quietly hoping to make a connection the

---

2. Howard Thurman, "Introduction," in *A Track to the Water's Edge: The Olive Schreiner Reader* by Olive Schreiner (New York: Harper & Row, 1973), xxvii–xxviii.

3. Howard Thurman, *With Head and Heart: The Autobiography of Howard Thurman* (New York: Harcourt Brace & Company, 1979), 9.

4. Howard Thurman, *Deep Is the Hunger* (Richmond, IN: Friends United Press, 2000), 212.

Eternal. Thurman considered a contemplative activity anything that brought us into an awareness of the Divine Presence, whether it be silence, liturgical dance, whirling, chanting, walking, poetry or literary reading, or an intense focus on a living Madonna. He began to incorporate many of these activities into his worship services in the 1930s. Yet he discovered that corporate or group silence was especially healing for him and his congregations.

This special emphasis on large group silence began during his study of mysticism with renown Quaker mystic and scholar, Rufus Jones. Thurman attended several Quaker meetings and sat in the silence that characterizes the unscripted forms of Quaker worship. In a 1951 sermon on corporate worship, later cited in *Visions of a Better World: Howard Thurman's Pilgrimage to India and the Origins of African American Nonviolence*, Thurman speaks of his experience with large group silence during a traditional Quaker meeting:

> Nobody said a word ... just silence. Silence. Silence. And in that silence I felt as though all of them were on one side and I was on the other side, by myself, with my noise. And every time I would try to get across the barrier, nothing happened. I was just Howard Thurman. And then ... I don't know when it happened, how it happened, I wish I could tell you, but somewhere in that hour I passed over the invisible line, and I became one with all the seekers. I wasn't Howard Thurman anymore; I was, I was a human spirit involved in a creative moment with human spirits, in the presence of God.[5]

Thurman wrote several volumes of meditations (e.g., *Deep Is the Hunger, Meditations of the Heart, The Inward Journey*) to facilitate these times of congregational silence before and as part of worship at Fellowship Church, San Francisco, and Marsh Chapel, Boston University.

---

5. Quinton Dixie and Peter Eisenstadt, *Visions of a Better World: Howard Thurman's Pilgrimage to India and the Origins of African American Nonviolence* (Boston: Beacon Press, 2011), 53.

There emerged a mystical unity between the meditation and the Sunday service of worship, making one creative synthesis. Perhaps the most amazing disclosure was the fact that, again and again, individuals who had scheduled appointments for counseling canceled, because in the total worship experience their needs had been met.[6]

He firmly believed that regular quiet time with God, contact with the Eternal is absolutely essential for spiritual growth, for truly living, for being alive in the world.

Thurman also engaged in what I like to describe as "creative silence." He paired himself with another person in another part of the country and they would "meet in the silence."

I would meet her in the silence, at exactly the same time twice each week, and we would be together in the presence of God. Each time I came home for a brief visit, we would share our experiences. Again and again we discovered that distance became more and more irrelevant. At last it seemed as if there was not distance separating us at all.[7]

Periods of stillness before and during worship service provided a healing spaciousness for Spirit to illumine and heal minds and created an atmosphere that stirred a sense of Presence in others. Likewise, Thurman intentionally attempted to spark a sense of Presence with his readings, sermons, music, and dance. He believed that spirituality could not be taught, but it could be caught—like a positive contagion.

Lives as a Holy Child of God

For most of his childhood, Howard Thurman lived with his grandmother, Ms. Nancy Ambrose, and his mother, Alice Thurman. In many publications, he recounts how Grandma Nancy bolstered the

---

6. Thurman, *With Head and Heart*, 160
7. Thurman, *With Head and Heart*, 159.

lagging self-confidence of her grandchildren as they became increasingly aware of their second-class citizenship. Born into slavery, Grandma Nancy shared with them the same tale repeatedly. Each year after the enslaved preacher was permitted to deliver a sermon to his enslaved neighbors, he would look each one in the eye and tell them, "You—you are not niggers. You—you are not slaves. You are God's children."[8] This proclamation enabled these enslaved individuals to cultivate a sense of dignity and worth based on belonging to God, and to all that God created. Their God-ordained worthiness was not subject to personal denigrations and social and physical restrictions. Knowing she was a holy child of God gave Grandma Nancy a sense of hope and an unbroken spirit during the savagery of slavery.

Thurman found the repetition of this tale uplifted their spirits and injected them with fresh vitality. Later he observed other children who had internalized the notion of being a holy child of God and made it central to their identity. They appeared to achieve far beyond what could be expected. Thurman later wrote, "The awareness of being a child of God tends to stabilize the ego and results in a new courage, fearlessness, and power. I have seen it happen again and again."[9] He also learned from Grandma Nancy that all strength and wisdom came from God. This knowledge of God being the Source of everything gave Thurman a sense of inner freedom which he attempted to ignite in others through his sermons and writings. For Thurman, being aware of your innate connection to God rooted you and spurred you to live from God. He often asked people this question: Who and what are you rooted in?

Cultivates a Curious Scrutiny

At the age of seven, Howard Thurman lost his father to pneumonia. Saul Thurman, an intellectual man and quite suspicious of organized

---

8. Howard Thurman, *Jesus and the Disinherited* (Boston: Beacon Press, 1996), 39.
9. Thurman, *Jesus and the Disinherited*, 39.

religion, did not attend the local Baptist church with Howard, his two sisters, mother, and grandmother. Young Howard felt baffled when the pastor refused to hold his father's funeral at the church and a visiting preacher who accepted the invitation condemned Saul to hell for "dying outside of Christ." Howard became bewildered by the eulogy and vowed never to attend church when he became an adult. Yet he continued to feel God's presence all around him as he walked through the nearby woods or rowed along the Halifax River.

When Thurman grew older, he began to scrutinize American Christianity to better understand why it castigated the unchurched. Wasn't character and virtue more important? As he delved more deeply, he observed that Christianity appeared to be a religion about Jesus rather than the religion that Jesus practiced on a daily basis. Thurman also noticed Christianity permitted slavery, colonialism, and imperialism. He believed the Gospels held another message from Jesus about love, intimacy with God, self-empowerment, the worship of God alone (instead of the idols of money, status, power, and celebrity). Thurman wrote about the road Jesus paved to inner freedom for those who like Jesus belonged to a dispossessed minority group in his classic book, *Jesus and the Disinherited*. This book nourished and stimulated people like Bayard Rustin, Pauli Murray, James Lawson, Martin Luther King Jr., and altered the course of American history.[10]

Another topic of inquisitiveness and exploration for Howard Thurman was the domain of mysticism. After he read *Following the Trail of Life*, written by the eminent Quaker mystic Rufus Jones, Thurman searched for an opportunity to meet and work with him. The childhood mystical experiences of Jones matched those of Thurman's early encounters with the Presence. Through a series of "holy coincidences," Howard Thurman was invited to study with Jones at Haverford College. Jones opened up his entire

---

10. Anthony C. Siracusa, *Nonviolence Before King: The Politics of Being and the Black Freedom Struggle* (Chapel Hill: University of North Carolina Press, 2021).

library to Thurman, who also participated in his seminar on mystics and mysticism. The seminar included a formal study of Meister Eckhart, St. Francis of Assisi, St. Teresa of Avila, St. John the Cross, French Quietist, Madam Guyon, among others.

Rufus Jones introduced Thurman to a distinction between negation mysticism (an isolated personal experience) and affirmation mysticism.[11] In affirmation mysticism, an individual goes down into Presence and comes up in community or oneness. In addition, affirmation mysticism stirs a certain moral or ethical concern in the individual. Quite intrigued with the possible implications that affirmation mysticism had for social transformation, Thurman expressed gratitude for this opportunity. However, he found that Jones held little respect for non-Christian mystics like Mahatma Gandhi nor did he apply affirmation mysticism to domestic issues like government sanctioned segregation and factory workers fighting for decent wages. Thurman notes:

> First, he helped me define and give a name to experiences that were part of my life ever since I can remember. Second, he introduced me to the concept of mysticism, which concept was completely foreign to my whole frame of reference. But when I got it, I had a handle now and a handle that is important. . . . The thing that I marvel at in Rufus was that in his presence you felt that you were in the presence of a great spirit, but in his presence, you felt that you were a great spirit. . . . I will always love him because he opened a way in my thinking and will always be identified with that way. I have no interest in whether my thoughts and his thoughts clash or are one; all that is irrelevant. But he opened up a way for my heart as the only other great teacher that I had opened up the way for my mind.[12]

---

11. For a more extensive discussion, see Howard Thurman, "Mysticism and Social Change: Rufus Jones," in *The Way of the Mystics*, ed. Peter Eisenstadt and Walter Earl Fluker (Maryknoll, NY: Orbis Books), 141.

12. Thurman, "Mysticism and Social Change," 158.

Thurman perceived the limitations in Jones's thinking and behavior while simultaneously noting how Jones as a contemplative leader carried a certain presence (of a great spirit) and drew the same presence (of a great spirit) from Thurman and other people he met and mentored. Some years later, friends and colleagues of Thurman would describe him similarly. Further, contemplative leaders like Thurman possess the ability to look past shortcomings to the gifts that are available to them in each moment.

Despite being admonished by black religious leaders for studying and writing about lofty matters such as mysticism rather than more liberating topics, Howard Thurman utilized mysticism to blaze an extraordinary trail toward social change. He saw mysticism as another form of religion and he set out to destigmatize words like "mystic" and "mysticism." He preferred the terms "religious experience" or "creative encounter." Thurman found it helpful to create categories of mystics (i.e., Christ mystics, intellectual, Light Within, and Associated with the Occult).[13] He felt that Presence can be discerned anywhere; in nature, during prayer or worship service and to anyone. Everyday mystics like Thurman or you or me live and work among us.

Models a Prophetic Spirituality and Sacred Activism

As Thurman uncovered a relationship between mysticism and social change, he knew he could assert a prophetic spirituality. He writes:

> Social action is an expression of resistance against whatever tends to or separates one from, the experience of God, who is the very ground of [his] being. . . . The mystic's concern with the imperative of social action is not merely to improve the conditions of

---

13. Howard Thurman, *Mysticism and the Experience of Love*, Pendle Hill Pamphlet 115 (Wallingford, PA: Pendle Hill Publications, 2015), Location 69.

society. It is not merely to feed the hungry, not merely to relieve human suffering and human misery. If this were all, in and of itself, it would be important surely. But this is not all. The basic consideration has to do with the removal of all that prevents God from coming to himself in the life of the individual. Whatever there is that blocks this calls for action.[14]

As early as 1929, Thurman began to speak about Jesus as the leader of a nonviolent religion and a noncooperator. He encouraged the black students at Spelman and Morehouse Colleges to not let anything crush their spirits, especially the frightful social environment they resided in and to seek succor from the Negro Spirituals, for in them lay hope-filled evidence of the Presence.

We are climbing Jacob's ladder;
We are climbing Jacob's ladder;
Every round goes higher, higher.

Have you ever heard a group singing this song? The listener is caught up in the contagion of a vast rhythmic pulse beat, without quite knowing how the measured rhythm communicates a sense of active belonging to the whole human race; and at once the individual becomes a part of a moving host of [human]kind. This is the great pilgrim spiritual.[15]

Later in 1936, Thurman, along with his wife, Sue Bailey Thurman, and Edward Carroll met with Mahatma Gandhi, who prompted them to be living examples of *ahimsa* (love or nonviolence) and *satyagraha* (civil disobedience or "holding on to the truth"). Upon his return from that pilgrimage to India in 1936, Thurman

14. Howard Thurman, "Mysticism and Social Action," Lawrence Lecture on Religion and Society, First Unitarian Church of Berkeley, October 13, 1978. Cited in Alton B. Pollard, III, *Mysticism and Social Change: The Social Witness of Howard Thurman* (New York: Peter Lang, 1992), 65.
15. Howard Thurman, *Deep River—The Negro Spiritual Speaks of Life and Death* (Richmond, IN: Friends United Press, 1975), 79.

continued to speak with fervor and write with increasing alacrity about the nonviolent religion he believed Jesus espoused in the Gospels. As he read, Thurman noticed a focus on the inward center or inner life of his oppressed people. Possessing control over one's inner life uplifts the spirit and provides the vigor needed to move against resistance to social change.

Although Howard Thurman was deeply concerned about alleviating the suffering and oppression of his own people, he felt there was a deeper call within contemplative or creative encounters. He felt that each time we have a religious experience or creative encounter, it should change us neurologically, emotionally, and eventually behaviorally.[16]

People frequently equate activism with demonstrations and marches. But not everyone involved in a social movement operates on the street. Many lawyers, ministers, cooks, childcare workers, teachers, community organizers, and journalists work tirelessly behind the scenes. Social justice work may include various forms of expression as a writer or essayist, poet, dramaturge, fine artist or sculptor, musician, athlete or architect. Nobel Prize winner Toni Morrison radically altered the publishing industry with her demands to expand the literary canons. Singers Billie Holiday and Nina Simone sacrificed their careers to bring attention to the egregious acts of violence toward black people in America. But how does activism become sacred?

Howard Thurman nudged and encouraged all who he quietly counseled to "Do what makes you come alive,"[17] "Follow the grain of your own wood,"[18] or "Listen for the genuine in you."[19] These

---

16. Howard Thurman, *The Creative Encounter: An Interpretation of Religion and the Social Witness* (Richmond, IN: Friends United Press, 1972).

17. Gil Bailie, *Violence Unveiled: Humanity at the Crossroads* (New York: Crossroads Publishing, 1995), xv.

18. Sam Keen, *To Love and be Loved* (New York: Bantam Books, 1999), 230.

19. Dr. Howard Thurman's Baccalaureate Address at Spelman College, May 4, 1980, as edited by Jo Moore Stewart for *The Spelman Messenger* 96, no. 4 (Summer 1980), 14-15.

phrases represented different ways of inviting Spirit to lead us to and in our sacred call and role in the restoration of God Beloved Creation. Thurman understood that social justice work is far more than righting wrongs or eliminating injustices. It is about removing the arbitrary and human-imposed barriers that separate us from each other and our oneness. He modeled contemplative leadership by listening for his evolving sacred call and urging others to do the same.

In every decision Thurman made, from cofounding an inter-denominational and interfaith church in San Francisco in 1944 to his acceptance of an appointment as the first black faculty member and dean of the Marsh Chapter at Boston University in 1953, he sought guidance from the Spirit as he listened for a "word in my heart."[20]

Walks with Inner Authority

One of many jewels of wisdom Howard Thurman leaves us with is the notion of inner authority. He alludes to its definition in his meditation, "The Inward Sea."[21] In this poem, Thurman refers to our inner sanctuary as an island within us that is guarded by angels. Insults or personal attacks cannot penetrate this sacred place unless they have the stamp of our approval, the consent of our inner authority. Asserting inner authority connects us with God.

Inner authority reflects our sense of agency, our ability to assess information, to make our own decisions and determine what we allow into our inner sanctuary. Thurman displayed inner authority throughout his life. As graduation from seminary neared, George Cross, his beloved seminary professor, told Thurman that he should abandon his concerns about social problems such as racial inequities and instead devote his mind and heart to feeding the timeless hunger of the human spirit. Thurman pondered deeply the words

---

20. Thurman, *With Head and Heart*, 169.
21. Thurman, *Meditations of the Heart*, 15.

of his professor, but knew that George Cross had no idea what it meant to live in a body of a man with black skin. Thurman chose to work on both fronts simultaneously because he knew they were interconnected.

Many people wondered why Howard Thurman did not pursue a PhD in religion. He possessed no desire to study an array of topics in religion unrelated to his interests. Thurman, utilizing his inner authority, knew he needed to follow the grain of his own wood and it led him to study and write about mysticism and social change.

When Howard Thurman chose to leave his tenured faculty position in the School of Religion at Howard University to cofound Fellowship Church without any financial guarantees to support his family, people condemned him and questioned his sanity. Thurman adamantly followed a vision he had in India to see if people from various denominations and racial and ethnic backgrounds could worship God under one roof. Again, he used his inner authority to weigh feedback and seek consultation in line with what he felt was his sacred call.

Thurman was also highly criticized for not being more actively involved as a marcher and organizer in the civil rights movement. He discerned that his gifts lie as a contemplative leader, one who would hold the spiritual space, spark the Spirit in others through his writings and sermons and to companion those who felt led to public protest. Thurman was not swayed by disapproval or praise and maintained a radical trust in God. He advocated that worry is evidence of a lack of trust in God.

With his life rooted in God, Howard Thurman incorporated Inner Authority to guide his life. He practiced deep and consistent inner listening, utilized spiritual discernment for decisions, and paid attention to divine interventions or the many sacred synchronicities that occurred on his spiritual journey. Thurman became a man inwardly led by Spirit rather than driven by fear.

Conclusion

I suspect it is impossible to detect a contemplative from physical appearance alone. Clearly they emerge from a wide array of racial or ethnic backgrounds, genders, and spiritual traditions. Unknowingly we may hold stereotypical depictions of contemplatives as individuals who walk slowly, speak gently, exude peace, and possibly wear flowing robes. But until we become acquainted with a contemplative leader, we may never know the depths of their thinking and being. We learn who they are by exploring the world inside of them. That inner world is often revealed in their writings, spoken words, or daily practices. And in their presence we may sense a loving Presence.

Once I encountered Howard Thurman, I felt affirmed for my early contemplative propensities and call to promote contemplative spirituality. As I began to meet increasing numbers of spiritual seekers attracted to the contemplative life, I realized that they sought role models. I love to expose them to Howard Thurman because he is an exemplar, a perfect prototype for contemplative leadership. Thurman set an inclusive, compassionate, and supportive tone everywhere he appeared. He often attracted followers because his deepest desire was to seek the Presence and to help others uncover their awareness of It in their own lives. Long after his physical death, we continue to feel his presence and the Presence he kindles in us with his words.

Contemplative leaders like Howard Thurman are aptly described by my spiritual director, Sophia Solomon, who commented, "They reflect the loving, deep, peaceful, free, compassionate presence of the Holy Spirit." It is a perfect description of Howard Thurman, who promoted contemplative prayer, commitment, growth in wisdom and spiritual maturity, and reconciliation as spiritual disciplines.[22]

---

22. Howard Thurman, *Disciplines of the Spirit* (Richmond, IN: Friends United Press, 1963).

Finally, Howard Thurman learned and mastered an essential principle articulated by Gerald May, one of the founding fellows of the Shalem Institute. May wrote about the poignant choice between being willful or willing.[23] Thurman who never described himself as a mystic, willingly submitted to God, an act all mystics must do. He writes, "The mystic yields the nerve center of his consent to a purpose or cause, a movement or an ideal, which may be more important to him than whether he lives or dies."[24] In an interview later in life, Thurman remarked, "When I was born God must have put a live coal in my heart, for I was his man and there was no escape."[25]

By yielding his very being to God, living as a holy child of God, protecting his inner sanctuary, promoting a prophetic, mystical spirituality, and walking with Inner Authority, Howard Thurman perpetually shows me and countless others how to live in the world but not be overcome by it. He understood that our spiritual growth is not for us alone. Every moment we spend in quiet time with God and other contemplative activities remind us of community, nudge us to remember our oneness with all of God's creation.

Howard Thurman left us with a treasure trove of eternal wisdom and nourishment that fertilize our deep spiritual yearnings and hunger through contemplative living and contemplative leadership. His spiritual prudence took him to a deep place which he expressed and shared in his many books and sermons. I will be forever grateful for his witness and clarion call to notice the aliveness, oneness, and wholeness in everything.

---

23. Gerald May, *Will and Spirit: A Contemplative Psychology* (New York: HarperOne, 1987).

24. Thurman, *Disciplines of the Spirit*, 17.

25. Jean Burden, "Meditation on Howard Thurman on the Occasion of His Memorial Service April 10, 1981," Howard Thurman Papers Project File, Boston University.

13

Considerations of Recovery, Centering Prayer, and Social Justice Action

Anita-Yvonne (AY) Bryant

Then the Lord God formed a man from the dust of the ground and breathed into his nostrils the breath of life, and the man became a living being.

(Gen. 2:7, NIV)

"I Can't Breathe."

—Eric Garner

n June 2015 I met with a group of mental health professionals and pondered what an adapted Alcoholics Anonymous (AA) twelve-step model of recovery might have to teach us about facing and addressing racial oppression.[1] We engaged each other and the potential utility of this model as we wrestled with the impact of the murders of Trayvon Martin and Eric Garner. In this essay, and this chapter of the nation's history, it is again time to reconsider

---

1. Anita-Yvonne Bryant, "Wa(o)ndering through Social Justice: One Step at a Time," Keynote Presentation at the Counseling and Consultation Services 75 Anniversary Celebration, Columbus, OH, June 2015.

the application of this framework alongside the Christian contemplative centering prayer tradition; again, pondering how the contemplative community might be nourished through the creation of individual and group practices that fuel social justice action. Structural oppressions are intertwined, yet the current focus is on racial oppression, an oppression that aligns with Thurman's understanding of the disinherited.[2] The beneficiaries of that oppression, the "misinherited" or majoritized communities, will also be centered.

On May 25, 2020, six years after Eric Garner uttered his final words, the United States (and many parts of the world) momentarily lost its breath. It viewed the eight minutes and forty-six seconds leading up to the murder of George Floyd by police officers. In June, Baker et al. reported on seventy cases in which the words, "I can't breathe" were spoken.[3] Some of these cases related to law enforcement brutality, others medical complications while under arrest. The centrality of the loss of breath will be explored further, later in this essay.

The time after Mr. Floyd's murder was identified as a national "racial reckoning." More precisely, it was a wake-up. Depending on one's social location, the disinherited woke up to another living nightmare. The loss of breath was one that accompanies community trauma, fear, terror, and rage. Those who are majoritized awakened to crushed beliefs about equality, fairness, public "safety," and feelings of guilt and helplessness, among many more reactions.

Some of these communities struggled to regain their breath. Steps were taken at the individual, community, and corporate levels. In communities of faith, there were opportunities to join congregational diversity working groups or engage in racial reconciliation processes between churches. People from Christian faith traditions flocked to

2. Howard Thurman, *Jesus and the Disinherited* (Boston: Beacon Press, 1996), 3.

3. Mike Baker, Jennifer Valentino-DeVries, Manny Fernandez, and Michael LaForgia, "Three Words. 70 Cases. The Tragic History of 'I Can't Breathe,'" *New York Times*, June 28, 2020, https://www.nytimes.com/interactive/2020/06/28/us/i-cant-breathe-police -arrest.html.

diversity and inclusion trainings, or provided these trainings for their churches and other places of worship. Ongoing reading groups and opportunities for spiritual formation were not uncommon. This was in addition to protesting and working to change systems structurally. These activities were an attempt to respond and promote social action and justice. For most, as the collective breath returned to its regular rate and rhythm; these activities could not be sustained.

Disinherited communities found themselves at the nexus of reaction, action, lament, and activation of racial traumatic stress alongside chronic experiences of racial oppression and activism.

Why Recovery?

Simply, a recovery model (in this case specifically the AA model), when adapted for racial oppression, allows for acceptance of racial oppression as a chronic individual, social, and structural condition. There is always work to be done altering its impact, yet it has no cure. The AA tradition is rooted in a spiritual invitation to reckon with how we, in our humanness, live with a chronic condition and disease while in community, engaging in life-long individual and systemic recovery processes. In recovery we come to accept that the transformative energy in our individual and institutional recovery, as it relates to racial oppression, is grounded in a power that is greater than ourselves.

The theologian Walter Wink speaks to this reality, stating:

> Any attempt to transform a social system (identified as the domination system) without addressing both its spirituality (spiritual influences) and its outer forms is doomed to failure. Only by confronting the spirituality of an institution and its concretions can the total entity be transformed, and that requires a kind of spiritual discernment and praxis that the materialistic ethos in which we live knows nothing about.[4]

---

4. Walter Wink, *Engaging the Powers: Discernment and Resistance in a World of Domination* (Minneapolis: Augsburg Fortress, 1992), 3.

This theme is again illuminated by theologian Jim Wallis:

Racism is rooted in sin—or evil, as nonreligious people might prefer—which goes deeper than politics, pointing fingers, partisan maneuvers, blaming, or name calling. We can get to a better place only if we go to that morally deeper place. There will be no superficial or merely political overcoming of our racial sins—that will take a spiritual and moral transformation as well. Sin must be named, exposed, and understood before it can be repented of.[5]

Finally, in *Alcoholics Anonymous: The Big Book*, it is stated:

The great fact is just this and nothing else: That we have had deep and effective spiritual experiences which have revolutionized our whole attitude toward life, toward our fellows, and toward God's universe. The central fact of our lives is the absolute certainty that our Creator has entered our hearts and lives in a way that is indeed miraculous. He has commenced to accomplish those things for us that we could never do by ourselves.[6]

There is an opportunity for majoritized communities and individuals to commit energy to not engage in the benefits derived from the disease of structural racism and racial oppression. Further, the wisdom gained in emphasizing the "day to day solutions" to managing racism as a chronic disease is at the nexus of God, the individual, and within a community context. There is power in reckoning daily with the chronic disease of racism for those that experience the significant benefits and opportunities of structural supremacy.

---

5. Jim Wallis, *America's Original Sin* (Grand Rapids: Baker Publishing Group, 2016), 33–34, Kindle Edition.

6. Anonymous, *Alcoholics Anonymous: The Big Book* (New York, NY: Alcoholics Anonymous World Services, 2002), 25.

One Step and Breath at a Time

To Jesus, God breathed through all that is . . . the time most precious to him was at the close of the day as this was the time for the "long breath."[7]

Disinherited and privileged contemplatives may choose to walk the adapted twelve steps of AA as they grapple with racial oppression. It is critical for the disinherited to understand the structural chains that bind and reduce access to life and liberty. Considering how these structures have an impact on individuals, relationships, and communities, it is essential to understand their simple complexity. Yet a common pitfall when initially doing racial recovery work cross-racially is that the disinherited may find themselves "under the gaze" of the majoritized, as this group seeks to learn about the lived experiences of the disinherited. Thus, for the purposes of this essay, centering the lived recovery experiences of those that derive benefits and advantages from the disease will serve as the ground for exploration.

Step One: We admitted we were powerless over alcohol—that our lives had become unmanageable.
Envision a scene where there is a weariness related to being embedded in and having advantages related to the workings of racial oppression. Walking into a meeting in a church basement or public library or into a small group of trusted colleagues, you find yourself saying, "I have a problem with the disease of racial inequality, and how I benefit from it. I increased my participation in learning groups and community outreach, yet my efforts are not fruitful. The more I do, the more I see and more frustrated I become. I want to change that."

What is immediately apparent is the community of fellowship. It lacks a sense of competing to be the top advocate and is marked

---

7. Thurman, *Jesus and the Disinherited*, 30.

by solidarity. Other beneficiaries of the privileges gained through the disease of racial oppression seem to be on a path, living a committed socially just and active life. Gathered there are people from different walks of life, yet they share a common commitment: living a socially just life in thought and deed and every day.

Step Two: Came to believe that a Power greater than ourselves could restore us to sanity.
Upon arrival at step two, Brooks challenges his readers to surrender their "Big Me." Brooks states, "What's lost is the more balanced view, that we are splendidly endowed but also broken."[8]

What is broken? Broken is running endlessly from community outreach to clothing drive to awareness dialogues to trainings and retreats. It is a hamster wheel driven by good intention, driven by compassion and concern, yet still a hamster wheel. This never-ending loop of activities, motivated by faith or guilt or charity, steadily decreases sanity and increases frustration and despair. The Creator may be acknowledged in these activities but remains at the periphery. Recognition of this facilitates real forward movement to the next step.

Step Three: Made a decision to turn our will and our lives over to the care of God as we understood Him.
Centering prayer offers light in the darkness as the privileged move into step three. Bourgeault[9] describes centering prayer as having the qualities of "intentionality, silence, surrender and return." Given the decision to turn life over to the Divine, God, the Creator, or Higher Power, centering down daily creates the necessary space to invite God in: what a possibility, over time, to experience

---

8. David Brooks, "When Cultures Shift," *New York Times*, April 17, 2015, https://www.nytimes.com/2015/04/17/opinion/david-brooks-when-cultures-shift.html.
9. Cynthia Bourgeault, *Centering Prayer and Inner Awakening* (Lanham, MD: Cowley Publications, 2004), 25, Kindle Edition.

that relational presence in increasing abundance in lifelong recovery. Thurman writes:

> I surrender myself to God without any conditions or reservations. I shall not bargain with him. I shall not make my surrender piecemeal, but I shall lay bare the very center of me, that all of my very being shall be charged with the creative energy of God.[10]

Step Four: Made a searching and fearless moral inventory of ourselves.

Step Five: Admitted to God, to ourselves and to another human being the exact nature of our wrongs.
The next two steps require both humility and courage for the exploration of how the advantaged contribute to and profit from racial oppression. Within the company of a trusted confidant, those contributions and profits are shared. There is growing awareness of contributions that uphold structural injustice and there are strong emotional responses related to that. The defects and defenses ensnare each other. The temptation to uphold racial inequality for the preservation of one's self becomes real. Many might reach a stumbling block at steps four and five. However, returning to centering prayer with intentionality, surrender, and return lights the path, breaks the silence, reduces the shame, and connects the privileged back to the larger community fellowship.

Step Six: Were entirely ready to have God remove all these defects of character.

Step Seven: Humbly asked Him to remove our shortcomings.
Laid bare, while supported by partners in recovery steps six and seven facilitate seeking God/The Higher Power for removal of the defects that uphold racial oppression. Again, it is written in *The Big Book*:

---

10. Howard Thurman, *Meditations of the Heart* (Boston: Beacon Press, 1981), 175.

If a mere code of morals or better philosophy of life were sufficient to overcome alcoholism, many of us would have recovered
long ago. But we found that such codes and philosophies did
not save us, no matter how much we tried. We could wish to
be moral, we could wish to be philosophically comforted, in fact
we could will these things with all our might—but the needed
power wasn't there to cure our alcoholism.[11]

Substituting "racial oppression" for "alcoholism," one can understand how these steps, by the grace of God, facilitate humility, soft-
ening of the heart, and openness to seeing for the first time the
impact of racial oppression on oneself and the disinherited.

*Step Eight: Made a list of all persons we had harmed and became will-
ing to make amends to them all.*

*Step Nine: Made direct amends to such people wherever possible except
when to do so would injure them or others.*
Steps eight and nine may present a challenge to the beneficiaries
of structural racism as they require addressing and making amends
to individuals. When there is an opportunity to make amends, the
apology should be specific and direct; taking accountability for
what harm was done. It is necessary to identify the impact of the
racial oppression at the individual and/or structural level and dis-
cuss what will change so that it doesn't happen again. When the
privileged are not able to identify a specific individual harmed by
the upholding of racial oppression, an adaptation of the discipline
of centering prayer might be considered.

In the preface to his book, Pennington[12] outlines instructions
for centering prayer learned from Thomas Keating that include a

---

11. Anonymous, *Alcoholics Anonymous: The Big Book,* 44–45.
12. M. Basil Pennington, *Centering Prayer* (New York: Crown Publishing Group,
2001), Kindle Edition.

sacred word that invites God's presence in, an introduction of that word, and when distracted, a return to the word, finally ending in a closing silence. The proposed adaptation, when direct amends cannot be made, uses a sacred breath instead of a sacred word. The sacred breath sets an intention not only for God's presence but the presence of the breaths that are extinguished in the lives of the disinherited daily. We return to the seventy cases investigated by *The New York Times*, where the words "I can't breathe" were uttered. The return to the breath invites accountability, and remembrance for those that no longer breathe; their lives taken by the disease of domination.

Step Ten: Continued to take personal inventory and when we were wrong, promptly admitted it.
By now, in partnership with God along with fellow participants in recovery, a process emerges of daily inventories. The daily commitment to illuminating and reducing participation in the individual and institutional pandemic of racism has a solid foundation upon which to sustain itself. Daily decision-making processes, and the values and behaviors that guide daily behavior, are assessed to determine how they spread racial oppression or reduce it. Benefits and advantages are weighed and reduced.

Step Eleven: Sought through prayer and meditation to improve our conscious contact with God as we understood Him, praying only for knowledge of His will for us and the power to carry that out.

Step Twelve: Having had a spiritual awakening as the result of these steps, we tried to carry this message to others, and to practice these principles in all our affairs.
The final two steps in the ongoing journey of recovery, steps eleven and twelve, are succinctly expressed in these three verses:

"Love the Lord your God with all your heart and with all your soul and with all your mind and with all your strength." The second is this: 'Love your neighbor as yourself.' There is no commandment greater than these."[13]

"I can do all things through Christ who strengthens me."[14]

These verses acknowledge the extension of the hand of fellowship to potential fellow sojourners. They also illuminate that incorporating recovery as a way of life is possible with the power of the Creator.

There will come a day, while traveling with fellow privileged sojourners, that those in recovery will come across another person strangled by their privilege. This person may have been discouraged by a workshop comment or endorsed a work policy that reduced access and increased barriers to maternal health care for the disinherited. Because they have not yet walked the steps, someone in the recovery group will stop, offer a welcoming hand, and say, "Hello I am _____. I too, wrestle with the advantages and benefits gained from the disease of racial oppression."

---

13. Mark 12:30–31 (NIV)
14. Philippians 4:13 (NKJV)

14

What Your Tender Heart Knows

Marcelle Martin

I n facilitating contemplative learning, it is a great gift to help
participants embody their spirituality more fully, so that they
can bring more of their whole, authentic being and expression
into all aspects of their lives. With experiential exercises, including
deep spiritual sharing, we can help participants open their hearts,
reveal themselves authentically, and experience the power of the
Spirit, which often manifests as love and insight. When serving
as facilitator, I have learned how crucial it is to pair intellectual
or informational content with experiential exercises and intimate
self-revelation. Wholeness and health require a good balance of
both the intellectual and the experiential. Offering broader perspectives and new knowledge can be greatly transforming, but
significant growth in the spiritual life often comes from direct
experiences and the sharing based upon those experiences. Helping people to connect with their felt experience and pay attention
to the knowing arising from the heart center is key to facilitating
experiences that awaken the heart.

Most people raised in Western cultures have been conditioned
since childhood to suppress certain kinds of bodily and spiritual
awareness and to focus our attention on what we can know with
our minds. An important part of the spiritual journey thus requires

practices that help us pay attention to our subtle spiritual senses and to the wisdom of our bodies. We need to learn to coordinate the wisdom of our brains with the wisdom that comes from the region of our bodies in which the heart is located, often called the heart center. Although we often think of the heart as being associated with emotions, in contemplative spiritual traditions focusing on the heart means attending to the subtle spiritual perceptions that we receive in this area. Episcopalian priest and contemporary author and teacher Cynthia Bourgeault writes:

> According to the great wisdom traditions of the West (Christian, Jewish, Islamic), the heart is first and foremost an organ of spiritual perception. Its primary function is to look beyond the obvious, the boundaried surface of things, and see into a deeper reality, emerging from some unknown profundity, which plays lightly upon the surface of this life without being caught there: a world where meaning, insight and clarity come together in a whole different way.[1]

To embody contemplative spirituality in our lives, we need to learn to listen in a deeper way to ourselves, to others, and to God. We are in need of practices and opportunities that help us give attention not only to our thoughts and emotions, but also to inner images, sensations, subtle movements of energy within, and spiritual perceptions. We can often grow more aware of ourselves in this way by becoming better listeners to others. When another person is sharing from the heart, we practice listening in an open, nonjudgmental way, paying attention not only to what others say, but also to how they say it and to the expressions and gestures of their bodies.

People are in great need of opportunities to share authentically and intimately with others. Having someone listen acceptingly while we speak from the heart helps us grow in our ability

---

1. Cynthia Bourgeault, "The Way of the Heart," *Parabola*, January 31, 2017, https://parabola.org/2017/01/31/the-way-of-the-heart-cynthia-bourgeault/.

to attend to our spiritual perceptions. Retreats, workshops, courses, and church groups often create opportunities for participants to share with each other in the whole group. Another level of intimacy can happen when some of the sharing is done in small groups and pairs. In very small groups and pairs, the ratio of speaking to listening is higher than when we speak in larger groups.

What and how participants share is key to whether or not they will be helped to access their spiritual perceptions, i.e., the knowing of the heart. It is therefore necessary to create experiences or offer prompts for sharing that elicit awareness of one's subtle perceptions and spiritual experiences. Experiential opportunities can include collectively engaging in a spiritual practice together, participating in a guided meditation as a group, creating a piece of art, reflecting on a deep spiritual truth or question while taking a walk, writing about an issue requiring deep contemplation, encountering nature with openness to divine revelation, participating in a ritual together, and more. When people gather after the experiential exercise, whether individual or communal, it is helpful to ask them to notice images and sensations that have arisen, as well as other subtle changes in their bodies and perceptions, and perhaps to write down what they notice. Then put participants in pairs or very small groups to share their experiences, with instruction to listen to each other with open, nonjudgmental attention.

We work with the assumptions: (1) that each person has a divine guide available directly within them (God, Christ, the Holy Spirit, the Inner Teacher); and (2) that when we listen to another person with confidence in their access to divine assistance, we help them strengthen their conscious connection to the divine Guide. Our role is to help people grow in their ability to access their subtle perceptions and their soul awareness, and to provide a space where people feel able to share their inner life in honest ways. It is crucial, therefore, for the partner or small group members not to offer interpretations of another person's experience or give suggestions.

Seeking Insights from the Heart

The questions that we offer can be key to the kind of sharing that happens. We want to give prompts that evoke spiritual awareness, rather than questions that elicit factual information or analytical reflection. It can be useful to talk about and model the difference between seeking answers or insight that comes from our mind and seeking answers or insight that comes through our hearts. When we direct prompts to our minds, we often elicit stories, ideas, analysis, or disembodied memories. When we offer prompts that evoke spiritual perceptions and the knowing of the heart, the responses that arise tend to have fewer words, more images, be more embodied, and include feeling along with truth. Before putting participants in pairs or small groups, it can be useful to model heartfelt responses.

"When do you experience the movement of the Spirit?" might be the prompt or question that is offered. When modeling sharing that comes from the heart, I often put my hand over my heart as I sense the knowing that is associated with that center in my body. Then I will speak it aloud, as an example: "Once in a while when I'm writing, I feel the flow of the Spirit moving through my body in a tangible way, sometimes flowing out of the top of my head like a fountain of energy."

When we feel safe in expressing our heart to our listener, we may take the risk to tell our listener things we rarely speak of in less intimate settings. "Sometimes when I'm caring about someone, I feel love and compassion flowing out of my heart toward them," I might say. "Sometimes what pours through seems like more than personal love; it's God's love flowing through me."

When a setting is created that helps people feel safe to share authentically, to tell the truth about their spiritual experiences and the perceptions of their hearts, we create a container for the Holy Spirit to work in powerfully healing ways, in individuals and in the group. In groups that become—even temporarily—communities where the work of the Spirit can take place freely, layers of restrictive social conditioning and armoring around the heart can gently be melted or peeled away, helping members of the group become more in touch with parts of themselves that they had walled off or pushed aside.

Facilitating the experience of their inner awareness and providing intimate sharing opportunities helps people give voice to truths that they have kept at the edge of their consciousness. Telling another person about our spiritual perceptions and embodied knowing releases tension in the body and frees frozen energy to move again. When grace is strongly present, participants glimpse more clearly the divine indwelling presence of God and Christ.

The Repeating Question

Many years ago, while participating in a long Buddhist meditation retreat, I experienced a practice that I have since used to great effect in the Quaker and contemplative retreats and programs that I facilitate. The practice is called the Repeating Question. The listener asks a question about the speaker's experience, a prompt intended for the heart. After the speaker responds, the listener says, "Thank you." Then, after a pause to reflect on what has been shared, the listener asks the question again. After each response, the listener says, "Thank you" and pauses to take in what has been shared. This continues for as long as the facilitator has set, which can be four or five minutes, or more. If participants have already practiced sharing responses that come from the heart—which tend to be briefer than those that come from the head—the question could be asked five, ten, or more times in five minutes. Then the two people switch roles. The new listener offers the question and listens lovingly to the response before saying, "Thank you."

When I offer this exercise in Quaker settings, I speak of the first Quakers, who often referred to people who were receptive to direct spiritual experience as "tender-hearted." At the end of a workshop or gathering, I like to use this form of the Repeating Question: "What does your tender heart know right now?" Before putting people in pairs, I point out that the question asks for the *knowing* of the heart, not the emotions. Of course, the knowing of the heart is often informed by emotions, but the question is seeking spiritual perceptions. The word "now" invites fresh sensing each time the question is posed.

Your Tender Heart

When a group of people has moved collectively to a space of deeper spiritual awareness and greater openness to authentic expression, the knowing that is available can be profound and sometimes surprising. When the question is offered gently, not as an interrogation but as an invitation, the divine wisdom that has become more available to participants during their time together often is evoked by this repeating question.

> "What does your tender heart know right now?"
> "My tender heart knows that it has a great deal to say and that it needs to be heard more often."
> "Thank you."

When our hearts are free to express themselves and coordinate with our minds, we become more whole people, and our spirituality becomes more embodied, as it was intended to be. Then we move through life with a greater sense of connection to all people, to society, to the earth, and to the whole cosmos. We also have a greater sensitivity and can receive a greater range of knowledge, including spiritual perceptions. The healing that is so needed in our time requires us to seek out and listen to the wisdom of our hearts.

15

Embodied Contemplation
of Deep Time
Resourcing for Spiritual Resilience
Kolya Braun-Greiner

"Grace happens when we act with others on behalf of our world."
—Joanna Macy[1]

Spiritual resilience is the capacity of our spirit and soul to be rooted, centered, and anchored in the Spirit of Life with an embodied sense of the transcendent Divine permeating all life with interdependence and interconnection. This is a theology expressed by Matthew Fox:

> What I'm about theologically is the replacement of theism with panentheism which is the idea that we're in God and God is in us. And by "we" I do not mean just humans, but all beings. The image I have is that the universe is the divine womb. We're all in here swimming together. It's an image of interconnectivity.[2]

---

1. "Joanna Macy: Living Spiritual Teachers: Quotes: Spirituality & Practice," Spirituality and Practice, accessed October 15, 2022, https://www.spiritualityandpractice.com/explorations/teachers/joanna-macy/quotes.

2. "Quotation by Matthew Fox," Spirituality & Practice, accessed March 23, 2023, https://www.spiritualityandpractice.com/quotes/quotations/view/282/spiritual-quotation.

These uncertain and turbulent times call for such spiritual resilience as we face the unprecedented suffering of the human and more than human world, caused by the androgenic desecration of Earth, a de-creation and great unraveling of the web of life, a thinning of the rich biodiversity our Creator breathed into existence about 14 billion years ago. Spiritual resilience can resource us to be flexible, enlivened, creative, courageous, and vulnerable, energies which lessen the immobilization of ennui, eco-anxiety, or existential dread. However, gaining this resilience is not merely an individual act of self-awareness and resourcing.

By engaging in this practice of deep contemplation, we also resource our wider community, human and more than human. We come to realize we are all one family of God the Creator, regardless of race, gender, or species, since we all come from the same source and cosmic story. When we contemplate this deep time, the awesome magnitude and beauty of it, we can discover our place in the universe story, ground ourselves in the wisdom of our ancestors, the interdependence of all life and thereby resourcing ourselves with spiritual resilience to enact our calling to know and tend Earth, rooted in our local environment. This wisdom, echoed in the mystical tradition of many faiths, knows we are not alone because of the inseparable interdependence we have with all life, calling us to be allies—with humans and as allies with the more than human beings and ecology of the natural world.

Mystical wisdom is incarnational, drawn from an embodied experience of witnessing the Spirit of Life in the tangible natural world and through whom "we live and move and have our being" (Acts 17:28, NRSV). The teachings supporting spiritual resilience do not present a hierarchical relationship of domination and oppression, as has been touted most especially from a white male dominated and colonized mindset of empire building. The wisdom sources which are not at the center of orthodoxy have also largely been ignored by the institutional church since it has often been hand in glove with that imperial mindset. Contemplation of teachings from the mystical tradition about our relationship with the whole evolutionary story of the universe and most especially with "Dear Mother Earth" (as Saint Francis said) offers a sorely needed antidote, one which is based upon a deeply relational nonhierarchical theology, rooted in experience rather than doctrine and connected to all life. This relational, familial understanding widens Jesus's admonition to "love our neighbor" to include not only our human neighbors but the more-than-human neighbors in our neighborhood. Our health and well-being are inextricably connected with our neighbors with whom we share our local ecology.

Meditation and Spiritual Sourcing

The following quotes as sources of meditation and spiritual resourcing all point toward a mystical wisdom which affirms that the transcendent Divine permeates all things, Earth, the natural world, with interrelatedness of one another and more than human life:

> **Hildegard of Bingen**, twelfth-century mystic, abbess, healer, and composer: "Holy Spirit, you are the mighty way in which everything that is in the heavens, on the earth, and under the earth, is penetrated with connectedness, penetrated with relatedness."[3]

> **Julian of Norwich**, fourteenth-century mystic and anchoress: "Nature and grace are in harmony with each other. For Grace is God and Nature is God. . . . God is the Ground, the substance, the same that is naturehood."[4]

> **Howard Thurman**, twentieth-century mystic, pastor, and author: "The earth beneath my feet is the great womb out of which the life

---

3. Matthew Fox, *Christian Mystics: 365 Readings and Meditations* (Novato, CA: New World Library, 2011), #23.

4. Fox, *Christian Mystics,* #40.

upon which my body depends comes in utter abundance. . . . In the contemplation of the earth I know that I am surrounded by the love of God."[5]

Sister Miriam Therese MacGillis, O.P., cofounder of Genesis Farm, and creator of the Cosmic Spiral Walk:[6] "The whole thing is grace. Everything of the Universe—everything that has brought forth the carbon in my body, my body itself, the trees that are shining outside my window, the bees that are flying around collecting pollen—it's all grace if we recognize it. It's there for us."[7]

Thomas Berry, C.P., twentieth-century mystic, "geologian," and scholar of world religions: "While we have recognized the inseparable nature of communion of God with the human community, we have not yet realized that this communion, to be perfect, must include communion with Earth. . . . The Body of Christ is ultimately the entire universe."[8]

The body of Christ is embodied! A contemporary expression of this wisdom can be discovered through an embodied practice of "Seeing with New/Ancient Eyes," the deep time of Earth's and humanity's story entwined with one another.[9] Seeing with

---

5. Howard Thurman, *Meditations of the Heart* (Boston, MA: Beacon Press, 1981), 210–11.

6. I attended workshops with Sister Miriam MacGillis held at Genesis Farm, New Jersey, and at Pendell Hill Retreat Center, Pennsylvania, where she introduced the Universe Story based upon the teachings of Thomas Berry. For an explanation of the Universe Story and its relevance for our times, see Sr. Miriam Therese MacGillis, "The Fate of the Earth, 1986," The Ecozoic Times, 1986, https://ecozoictimes.com/resources/articles-2/the-fate-of-the-earth-miriam-therese-macgillis-1986-2/.

7. "Genesis Farm: Restoring Paradise: One Watershed at a Time," Kosmos Journal, September 20, 2016, accessed March 24, 2023, https://www.kosmosjournal.org/news/genesis-farm-restoring-paradise-one-watershed-at-a-time/.

8. Thomas Berry, *The Christian Future and the Fate of the Earth*, ed. Mary Evelyn Tucker and John Grim (Maryknoll, NY: Orbis Books, 2012), 11.

9. Seeing with New/Ancient Eyes is the third stage of the four-stage process of the Work That Reconnects, of which Joanna Macy (the opening quote) is the root teacher. The four stages are: Coming from Gratitude, Honoring Our Pain for the World, Seeing with

"new/ancient eyes" occurs through contemplation and embodied experience when we hear the voice of Earth, other living beings, our ancestors, or future beings speaking through us. Such awareness can come to us as a slow awakening or as a sudden epiphany of an "Ah-Hah!" moment when we discover our deep interconnectedness and interdependence with all life.

A contemplative embodied experience of deep time offers two "axes" for resourcing ourselves with new/ancient eyes with which to "face the mess we're in."[10] Imagine a circle in which your life is at the center of the circle of life, with two lines passing through the center, one horizontal and the other vertical. The horizontal line depicts shows the long history of deep time as the evolutionary story before and after your life (or that of humanity), of *deep interconnectedness or interrelatedness* with the whole of Creation.

The horizontal (nonhierarchical) evolutionary storyline tells repeated chapter themes showing of the power of Earth to heal and keep generating life in spite of tremendous odds. There have already been five major mass extinctions and now due to human activity we are:

> on the brink of a sixth mass extinction, comparable to the one that wiped out the dinosaurs ... [shown by] a study, which calculates that three-quarters of today's animal species could vanish within 300 years.... The silver lining in this dark cloud is that if humans work quickly to protect endangered and threatened

New/Ancient Eyes, and Going Forth. They are described here: https://workthatreconnects .org/spiral/. The third stage of Seeing with New/Ancient Eyes offers us a tangible experience of our intimate relationship with all that exists. We come to a new or renewed awareness that the wider world, created by the Divine Source of all life, can support and empower us. Our relatedness spans past and future generations along with the more than human world. With respect for this relationship can speak on behalf of and be in solidarity with the more than human world as fellow members of the web of life we share in common.

10. Joanna Macy and Chris Johnstone, *Active Hope: How to Face the Mess We're in with Unexpected Resilience and Creative Power* (Novato, CA: New World Library, 2022), 7.

species and their habitats now, the mass extinction can be prevented or at least delayed by thousands of years.[11]

Since all life on Earth is interrelated and interdependent, our survival as a human species is threatened too. Rooting and grounding ourselves in the sacredness of the evolutionary story can awaken us to gratitude, a motivation to support the "thrival" of all life with whom we are deeply connected. This story shows that we are indebted to lives that preceded our appearance as Homo sapiens in Africa, a mere 500,000 years ago. Our genetic inheritance of this story line shows up in the fact that we share most of our DNA in common with other animals, and even many plants. What indigenous peoples and mystics have known for generations is now being proven by science—we are all related.

A common refrain during Native American prayers is "all my relations," as a way of honoring this deep relatedness. Robin Wall Kimmerer, a Potawatomi botanist, teaches that creatures are part of the same family with us.[12] Wisdom from these more than human relatives too long ignored by the dominant culture is found in Book of Job: "Ask the animals

and they will teach you" (Job 12:7, NRSV). The evidence from the long trajectory of the deep time evolutionary story seems to point to this wisdom: All life is interrelated and wants to keep on "life-ing." In the language of Christian faith; God is life-giving power, the Spirit of Life overcoming death.

The vertical "axis" offers deep *interdependence* with other beings and with other generations, ancestors and future generations.[13] The

11. Ann Gibbons, "Are We in the Middle of a Sixth Mass Extinction?" Science, March 2, 2011, https://www.science.org/content/article/are-we-middle-sixth-mass-extinction.

12. Robin Wall Kimmerer, "Robin Wall Kimmerer, Reciprocity," YouTube (Western Colorado University School of ENVS, November 9, 2017), https://www.youtube.com /watch?v=wisxnOgOlFo.

13. I have chosen for this axis a vertical orientation because we "stand on the shoulders of those who go before us."

wisdom our ancestors offer us is accompanied by the wisdom from the "eyes of the future looking back at us, and they are praying for us to see beyond our own time," as Terry Tempest Williams has declared.[14] This deep time intergenerational connection can be a source of wisdom for intergenerational solidarity informing how we live on Earth and could be expressed as "choose life so that you and your descendants may live" (Deut. 30:19, NRSV).

Caring for the seven generations, past, present, and future is a worldview common to Native American traditions. "It's timely that we consider sustainability and as we prepare for the generations coming after us."[15] The deep interconnectedness of all beings seen through new/ancient eyes is also resonant with what the Buddhists call "Interbeing," or all things "inter-are."[16] We also hear these themes within the largely ignored Wisdom (called by Sophia in Greek) tradition of Judaism and Christianity. Some examples:

All wisdom is from [God],

and with [God] it remains forever.

The sand of the sea, the drops of rain,

and the days of eternity—who can count them?
    (Sirach 1:1–2, NRSV)

Wisdom was created before all other things,

and prudent understanding from eternity.

The root of wisdom—to whom has it been revealed?
    (Sirach 1:4–6, NRSV)

---

14. Terry Tempest Williams, *Refuge: An Unnatural History of Family and Place* (New York, NY: Random House, 1991).

15. Ron (Deganadus) Lester, "Seven Generations," YouTube (YouTube, May 18, 2017), https://www.youtube.com/watch?v=wHg3enCCyCM.

16. For example, in the apple we can "see" the sun, rain, soil, the bee that pollinated it and the person whose hands harvested it. See Thich Nhat Hahn, "What Is Interbeing? (by Thich Nhat Hanh)," Rina G. Patel, September 2, 2016, https://www.rinagpatel.com/blog2/2016/9/2/what-is-interbeing-by-thich-nhat-hanh.

[Wisdom] reaches mightily from one end of the earth to the
other,
and she orders all things well. (Wisdom 8:1, NRSV)

Can you witness the eternal Wisdom (Sophia) of God expressed
permeating the tangible elements of the wider world of Earth and
all things created in the deep time story of Creation?

The wisdom drawn from our evolutionary roots as well as
ancestral tradition offers resources for spiritual resilience that are
sorely needed for these times of climate crisis and environmental injustice. These sources of wisdom offer strength, solace, and
courage—the kind of deep grounding that people are yearning for.
This yearning for deep connection can be expressed as solidarity
through equity and justice for all life (not only humans).

Embodied Contemplative Practice of Deep Time:
An Evolutionary Spiral Walk

An embodied awareness of the two realms or axes (interdependence
inherited from the evolutionary story and interconnectedness with
ancestral and future beings) of "Seeing with New/Ancient Eyes"
can be experienced through a contemplative walking meditation on
the Spiral Evolutionary Walk, traversing the 13.7 billion year history of the universe.[17] This ritual practice can be offered at a retreat
or congregation setting for youth and/or adults as a standalone ritual activity or as an activity within a class on spiritual resilience
to act on behalf of future life or as part of Work That Reconnects
workshop. Organizers of this experience are encouraged to weave

---

17. My version is adapted from Sr. Miriam Therese MacGillis who founded the Genesis Farm. A setting on fairly level ground offers an enhanced experience of being surrounded by the natural world. In lieu of ability to walk the spiral, one can follow the spiral
on paper with one's finger as a meditation, slowly traversing the nearly 14 billion year
story (with a 70" piece of string shaped or a line drawn into a spiral with 5 circuits around,
about ¾" apart with about 8" for each billion years) can give a sensation how incredibly
long it took for all stardust to manifest as life.

in teachings from their own faith tradition that complement the deep time story of Creation and our role in it. While an individual can meditate upon the chronology of evolution and wisdom of intergenerational history, an individual experience of spiritual resilience is magnified when this embodied contemplative practice is collectively experienced along with a shared "harvesting" of "new/ancient eyes" awareness together. This new consciousness and heightened awareness often lead people to be more motivated to be active healers of their community environment.

Imagine entering a large room and seating yourself with others around a path spiraling out from the center of the room, which is dimly lit by candles placed at intervals along the spiral. Also along the spiraling 140 foot path representing the nearly 14 billion year story of our universe, God's Creation, are images depicting the creation of stars, nebula, and galaxies (from the Hubble space telescope).[18] After the first 10 billion years, the birth of our sun occurs, so our subsequent solar system, formed with our Dear Mother Earth, is depicted. During the next 1 billion years, a flourishing of images appears along the spiral, sequencing the abundant emergence of life. Humanity's first ancestors appear about 500 million years ago (the last 6 inches of the 140-foot spiral), among the most recent actors upon this beautiful blue-green planet.[19] A center candle is lit and you hear these words from Genesis 1:3 spoken: "Let there be Light and there was light," with a great flaring forth (NRSV). Meditative music of a "cosmic/space music" genre is heard quietly in the background as one by one (and spaced a few minutes apart), people enter the center and embark on this

---

18. A walkable exhibit of this universe story is on display at the American Museum of Natural history in New York City. See "Cosmic Pathway: A Walkway Depicting 13 Billion Years: AMNH," American Museum of Natural History, accessed October 13, 2022, https://www.amnh.org/exhibitions/permanent/cosmic-pathway.

19. For the timeline, sample script, Hubble images, and other resources you can adapt, see "Cosmic Walk, an Interactive Ritual," Worship Words, June 3, 2020, https://worshipwords.co.uk/the-cosmic-walk-sister-miriam-therese-mcgillis-usa/.

walking meditation, traversing slowly around and around the spiral, through nearly 14 billion years, noticing with their bodies the incredible timespan it took for life to appear on Earth, very near the end of the spiral where we stand now in the present moment of Creation and evolutionary history.

Harvest of Seeing with New/Ancient Eyes

When groups engage in Evolutionary (or Cosmic) Spiral Walk, some of the discovered or recovered wisdom shared have been:

* Enabling of the spirit. Importance of feeding spirit and joy.
* Widening the mind to include the rainforest.
* The importance and power of ritual—expressing the nonverbal.
* Feeling more grounded—How can one be in the world this way?
* Self-care practice for activists.
* Imagination has power.
* Even as an elder, bloom where you are planted. You have more impetus for action.
* Feeling at one with Creation inspires action, rather than running away due to the overwhelming nature of the problems we face.
* Enlarges one's vision of being alive right now. Through the shared experience one feels more connected to the community.

The experience of an embodied existential cosmology can be practiced in the wider world, in our daily lives, in the moments we encounter other beings in our comings and goings, with renewed understanding and gratitude that we are all from the same Source of Life, interrelated and interdependent. Contemplating this cosmology most often awakens a deep sense of awe and wonder at both the exquisite beauty and terror, both the glory and the suffering within the deep time story of life's emergence time and time again in spite of death. Renewed hope is found based upon the embodied experience of walking through the cosmic story, which confirms that the Spirit of Life is stronger than death. Along with hope arising, a profound humility is felt in relationship to the exquisite biodiversity of Creation, that we "stand on the shoulders" of so much life that has gone before us which is available to teach and guide us forward into a Great Turning toward a life-sustaining future. Thus being resourced with spiritual resilience, fueled by awe, wonder, and humility, people have more inspiration and motivation to act with reverence on behalf of life.

A benediction: It took 14.5 billion years for stardust to form the unique being that you are. The Spirit of Life must have a purpose for you being here. God or Spirit of Life wants us to keep on living. Embodied with such assurance and spiritual resilience, may you find the strength to enter into a quest for justice defending human and the whole web of life so that future generations may live.

16

A Contemplative View of Resilient Aging

Elaine Voci

n 2023, more of us will live into our nineties, and we are likely to meet our share of active centenarians. Medical research continues to increase our understanding of healthy aging. We are learning that "successful aging" is not an oxymoron, but a beacon of hope and light, and that awe and wonder don't have a time stamp.

The ageist assumption that adults sixty-five and older have little to look forward to, and are unable, or unwilling, to adapt to change denies the reality of elders who have overcome challenges for decades. They have faced significant losses and have made numerous life transitions, many that required starting over, such as changing jobs and careers, moving to new geographic locations, or losing partners to illness or divorce. They have provided decades of responsible caregiving, first for their young children, then for elderly parents, and, finally, for spouses suffering from dementia and other serious illnesses. In spite of all that, many are *thriving*, not just surviving. They are resilient, a term I use to describe being able to overcome the unexpected stressors in life, both light and dark, to see past them, and to continue to find enjoyment.

Within this larger group of wise elders, there are those of us who are "contemplatives," and we share similar life experiences with our elder peers. But our resiliency has been strengthened by the daily devotion to spiritual practices that enrich our lives, especially centering prayer and holding reverence for time spent in nature, in stillness, and in solitude. These practices expand our capacities for coping with challenges and foster a beneficial inner peace and renewal that contribute to our well-being.

I define contemplatives as those who hold their hearts in prayer, and turn to prayer when making the myriad decisions of life. In Rose Mary Dougherty's powerful little book, titled *Discernment, A Path to Spiritual Awakening*, she reflects on prayer that is "abiding prayer; the intention of freedom for love; the intention of compassionate action; the intention of living my true identity, abiding in love."[1]

The pilgrim's path to God comes with twists and turns unique to each person's life story. At some point in their journey, contemplatives feel a yearning to form a deep and meaningful relationship with God that cannot go unanswered. As Howard Thurman wrote in *Meditations of the Heart*:

> Always there is the persistent need for some deep inner assurance, some whisper in my heart, some stirring of the spirit within me—that renews, re-creates and steadies.
>
> Then whatever betides of light or shadow, I can look out on life with quiet eyes. God is with me.[2]

In my own life story, my yearning for God was amplified during a near fatal auto accident in which I left my body and entered another realm where I was met by a silent monk who telepathically communicated with me, and guided me to visit a Great Hall of Records. After being presented with my book of life to briefly examine, I was given a choice to exercise my free will: I could either die in this accident, or I could return to my life with

---

1. Rose Mary Dougherty, *Discernment* (Mahwah, NJ: Paulist Press, 2009), ix.
2. Howard Thurman, *Meditations of the Heart* (Boston, MA: Beacon Press, 1953), 48.

an understanding that there would be certain necessary changes to be made. I was told that there was no "right" or "wrong" choice; either would be accepted. During this extraordinary encounter, I was shown that life on earth is a giant school in which we are learning to love unconditionally, in the same way that we are loved by God. I chose to come back and finish raising my two sons, who were nine and eleven years old at the time, all the while trusting in the certain knowledge that God was always with me and that I would be helped to grow into the new life that awaited me.

The Beloved Partnership

Contemplatives live authentically with God as their companion, and that relationship is at the center of their being, and is the basis for how they live, think, and respond to daily life. As a group, we share many qualities; here are five that I have noticed in myself and my contemplative peers that give expression to this Beloved Partnership:

- A Shift from Ambition to Meaning
- Loving Their Work as Their Calling
- Guided by a Reflective Philosophy
- A Joyful Generativity
- Creativity and the Artist's Rule

From Ambition to Meaning

As a worldwide population, those over the age of sixty-five consistently remain among the happiest of all age groups, and many actually *like* being older. A shift in midlife from ambition to meaning enables them to look at growing old as a privilege, and as a new stage of life with its share of pleasures and perils. With a positive outlook and a sense of gratitude, they adapt to the inevitable changes of aging with resilience and skillfulness. When they encounter suffering along the way, it adds depth to the meaning and purpose of their lives. Knowing that life can be hard only sweetens the appreciation of life's joys, and its tender moments.

It has been my experience that I and my contemplative friends and colleagues made that shift during our fifties and sixties, and it served to enhance our commitment to companion with God. After my contemplative friend Bob took early retirement from an executive position in a large company, he explained to me over a coffee chat:

> My whole life changed after that, and I revisited all of my habits. I slowed down and listened to my life, and to what God helped me discern as my next steps. I became aware that I wanted the rest of my days to focus on building good memories with my family; on daily meditation and prayer; and a few good causes to which I give my time, talent, and money. Today, I am older with a peaceful heart, and savoring each day.

In graduate school, I met a paraplegic named Tom when I interviewed him for a medical research study of men with spinal cord injuries. Tom's life had been disrupted after a diving accident left him paralyzed and in a wheel chair. He told me the inspiring story of his inner transformation, and described an uncanny and pivotal turning point during his initial hospitalization. He met a young pastor who was assigned to meet new patients and who prayed with him; he spoke in a way that was comforting and reassuring. The pastor mirrored a steadfast love of God, a love that was constant, and faithful. He taught Tom to quiet his mind and body so that he could hear God's voice within, something that Tom described as "spiritual food" for his struggling soul. He regarded the pastor as God's direct intervention in his life, at a time when his need was great, and his faith was badly shaken.

Tom told me that he gradually came to view his injury as an "inconvenience," and realized that "everyone was disabled in some way." He crafted a new life that included being hired by a global manufacturing company, finding a faith community where he and his wife became active members, and starting a family. Tom's spiritual transformation fueled a passion for speaking to spinal cord–injured patients in the local rehab hospital, where he reassured them that a good life doesn't depend on being able-bodied, and that with God as your companion, a life of meaning and purpose was within reach, ready and waiting for them.

Loving Their Work as Their Calling

Contemplative elders are busy people; many continue to work at a vocation they love and feel called to, such as Quaker writer Parker Palmer, who wrote a reflective memoir, *On the Brink of Everything*, when he turned eighty. He asserts, "Old age is no time to hunker down, unless disability demands it. Old is just another word for nothing left to lose, a time of life to take bigger risks on behalf of the common good."[3]

Some contemplatives retire and then return to their field when a new need arises, or an unexpected crisis occurs and they feel called to contribute. As my friend, hospice executive and nurse Penny Davis, observes in her latest book, *The Balance Project*, "Just when I thought that I was retiring a few years ago, I began a new journey with a homeless hospice project. Now, four years later, I'm proud that we are serving patients that are desperate for quality end-of-life care.... I'm old enough to know what I'm doing and young enough to still want to do it."[4]

In my own elderhood, I retired from a private coaching practice, while keeping some hours for a few long-term clients who return periodically. I devote time to a new and gratifying ministry

---

3. Parker Palmer, *On the Brink of Everything* (Oakland, CA: Berrett-Koehler Publishing, 2018), 2.
4. Penny Davis, *The Balance Project* (Northampton, NH: Mindstir Media, 2022), xiv.

that inspires me: caring for several of my neighbors. One is an older man suffering from Parkinson's disease; I visit with him every other week, and I spend time with his wife to provide emotional support as he gradually loses ground. I also care for a neighbor who is a nurse, and, until recently, worked the night shift for years at a nearby city hospital; we enjoy cooking for one another periodically, and sharing conversations about life. Finally, there are new neighbors who just moved here this summer; Rasheed and his wife are medical scientists working in a research study of coronary artery disease; I recently hosted a porch party where a few neighbors helped me welcome them over a freshly baked apple pie and hot cider.

My ministry provides practical services to others, and brings me a feeling of being used for the greater good, one of the best feelings in the world. As an elder, I have the time to serve, the desire to relieve suffering in the world, and the conscious intention to leave a legacy of love. My own grandchildren and adult children no longer need me in the same way that they once did, and I am blessed with energy in abundance, so it seems fitting that God inspired me to begin this spiritual endeavor.

A Reflective Philosophy of Life

Elderhood is a journey of the human spirit. As writer Joyce Rupp teaches in *Praying Our Goodbyes,* it is a journey that comes from inside the "pilgrim heart . . . a part of us that is never home, that is always stretching and yearning to be home but knows that we have not yet arrived."[5]

Elderhood is also a developmental stage of the human life cycle that contains unexpected transitions, unavoidable losses, and events that generate humility; the one thing that can be predicted

---

5. Joyce Rupp, *Praying Our Goodbyes* (Notre Dame, IN: Ave Maria Press, 2009), 45.

about growing old is the unpredictability of life. Contemplative elders accept life's impermanence. Knowing that life is "on loan" is understood as a sacred gift, one given in great love. Such acceptance develops both the capacity for joy and gratitude while also enabling them to hold people, places, and things lightly, without clinging.

Elders practice centering prayer, which fosters inner peace. Howard Thurman wrote about this in his book *Meditations of the Heart*, and he spoke of "centering down ... to sit quietly and see one's self pass by."[6] I am currently a student in Zoom-based contemplative classes, and I and my classmates are able to glimpse how our reflective teachers live; we cannot help but notice the backdrop of fresh flowers, living plants, books, and colorful talismans located around their rooms. These are silent teaching tools that convey a contemplative philosophy that cherishes learning and the pursuit of wisdom, along with a devotion to beauty that draws our souls toward the Creator.

Contemplatives view hope as something to be cultivated from within, and an important resource that builds resilience when life is hard. Hope is not a denial of what is real, or a panacea of magical powers. As Gerald May teaches in *The Awakened Heart*, "Try to let your responses flow out from your heart rather than take the place of your heart. ... Turn your heart toward the source, and offer your hope."[7]

I experienced the power of hope to transform darkness into light when I counseled alcoholics and drug abusers in treatment programs during my early career. A frequent prescription given to patients was to go for a walk on the grounds, find a bench under a tree on which to sit, and to journal their inner thoughts and feelings. Even if the skies were not always blue and the sun was not

---

6. Thurman, *Meditations of the Heart*, 28–29.
7. Gerald May, *The Awakened Heart* (New York: HarperCollins, 1991), 89.

always shining, the energy from the natural world had the power to transform the ordinary into the sacred. Clients, even those who had so often felt hopeless in their addiction, would speak about finding a "Higher Power" and being reassured by the flowers, trees, and the birds' singing that life was worth living.

Generativity

Generativity refers to a stage of elderhood in which older adults willingly and intentionally nurture others, especially the younger generation, and pass their wisdom down through grandparenting, volunteering, mentoring, community activism, and teaching. Generativity is an instinctual life-giving activity that is rooted in a bedrock of hope and love, a gathering of graces leading to spiritual freedom and growth toward God.

Over the past two years, I have been nurtured by a number of silver-haired contemplative teachers in their seventies and eighties whose passion for generativity is obvious in their enjoyment of helping others learn. One of the most memorable teachers I met is Judith Favor, an accomplished and warm-hearted octogenarian who has been guiding contemplative writing classes and retreats since the 1970s. I studied contemplative listening and writing with her for a year. She made me feel safe and supported as she modeled undivided attention and kindness to her students.

Her insights were both practical and enlightening, as demonstrated in the following example: The topic was showing hospitality to the stranger and how it relates to the spiritual discipline of contemplative listening. During our breakout sessions, she explained, we might feel awkward with people we don't know, and it could foster self-doubt as we practiced listening. She encouraged us by sharing these comforting observations,

> You and I are called to practice hospitality in chaotic times, so take courage.... Hospitality to yourself preserves your inner

freedom and strengthens your agency, so you are never cowed or bowed by the behavior of others. Hospitality calls us to put one foot in front of the other, lifting each other up all along the way.[8]

Bolstered by her wise guidance, we went on to our practice sessions feeling uplifted and alive.

Creativity and The Artist's Rule

Contemplative spiritual practices support the pursuit of a creative life, and having a "rule of life" is a practice from ancient times that suits modern artists. According to Christine Valters Paintner, a rule of life is a "set of wisdom guidelines for how to live in a meaningful way."[9]

Rather than a rigid set of actions, a rule of life utilizes self-discipline and sustainable guidelines that offer practitioners a balance between the competing human drives for structure and freedom. Having sufficient structure allows us to be challenged by the practice and grow from it, while having the freedom to nourish and invite our creativity to thrive. As she explains,

> [T]here are certain in rhythms to my life that are essential for my creative energy. These include writing each morning, walking to care for my body, letting my energy shift out of my head for awhile, knowing when to let go and let something incubate, and getting adequate rest and play.[10]

Creativity is the natural order of life and when contemplatives open themselves to it, they believe that they are opening themselves to the Creator's creativity in them. They view creativity as another of God's gifts, knowing that it is meant to serve the

---

8. Judith Favor, "Contemplative Writing and Listening Practice Group," Spirituality & Practice, e-course, class notes, April 16, 2021.

9. Christine Valters Paintner, *The Artist's Rule* (Notre Dame, IN: Soren Books, 2011), 5.

10. Paintner, *Artist's Rule*, 152.

world. In her best-selling classic book, *The Artist's Way*, author Julia Cameron declared, "The heart of creativity is an experience of the mystical union. . . . You are seeking to forge a creative alliance, artist-to-artist with the Great Creator . . . and when we move out on faith into an act of creation, the universe is able to advance."[11]

There is a reason why so many contemplative people are creative artists, writers, poets, musicians, singers, and teachers; their artistic pursuits are an expression of their spirituality. The skills needed for making art are the same as those needed for spiritual growth, such as listening for inspiration, silence, and reflection. Contemplatives find direction, perspective, and resilience through art and creativity.

I use daily rituals as a rule of life for my creative work; upon entering my home office, I light a candle, and invite Spirit to be with me as I coach, write, and create. This simple ritual signals to me that I am here to give meaning and significance to my actions and that I am working with mindful awareness. It also separates me from what I do elsewhere. It brings me to a quiet, receptive, and creative state of mind to begin my work for the day.

I also use ritual when I facilitate a bimonthly grief support group held at a local church. I intentionally prepare the meeting room by creating a space in which participants will feel safe and comfortable and that will honor our conversation. I bring flowers and a beautiful mandala tablecloth upon which I place various talisman such as an angel, a painted heart, and a crystal pyramid. These items represent hope, faith, and love; they invite reflection and inspiration and bless the space we will occupy in our gathering.

When everyone has arrived, I welcome them and invite them to pray with me as I read a short psalm and words of encouragement to open our gathering. This ritual silently performs an important

---

11. Julia Cameron, *The Artist's Way* (New York: Jeremy P. Tarcher/Putnam Books, 1992), 2.

service by acknowledging the inner change that each attendee is going through in their grief, while the physical setting and supportive process brings comfort and builds emotional resilience.

Contemplative Elders of the Future

I believe that contemplative elders have the capacity to serve as unapologetic change agents for a better world in the future. The level of consciousness on our planet is expanding and we can find abundant evidence that we are all connected to one another. There are no passengers on this spaceship: We are all crew members. We are approaching the time when we must feed the field with more love, kindness, compassion, and caring for each other if we are to avoid global disaster and make an evolutionary leap. This is our choice and our destiny.

Contemplative elders can help lead the way by showing their courage, love, compassion, and solidarity to help humanity shift the current societal paradigm from the love of power to the power of love. In the visionary writing of Judy Cannato's beautiful, and final, book, *Field of Compassion*, she powerfully frames this transition by reminding us that

> We live in a world of grace, and as we more consciously receive grace, each of us becomes a Field of Compassion. Each one of us becomes open to love a little more completely, and then love pours out of us and into the world. As we become free, others experience freedom in our presence, and can choose to be open to love, too. This is our life work, our great work, what the Universe asks and what this moment in time demands.[12]

We become what we practice. As contemplative elders we are well disciplined in our practices, but we will need new hearts to accompany us on our way to the future that Judy imagined. Let us pray:

---

12. Judy Cannato, *Field of Compassion* (Notre Dame, IN: Soren Books, 2010), 191.

I need a new heart, God, filled with hope for the world I live
   in now
and conviction for the one I will occupy in coming days.
Let me not shirk from my sacred duties,
let me dare to join hands with fellow pilgrims
to walk a path of radical transformation.
Fill me with joy and faith that I may be inspired to be bold
   and brave,
to lift others as I climb,
and to share this unfolding miracle story with the world.
Create in me a spirit of peace;
take my heart and renew it with your goodness and mercy,
that I may bring a legacy of love in Your Name.
Amen.

17

Summer Day of the Owls

DanaLee Simon

have always loved the natural world. My mother's people were farmers—hands-in-the-dirt-soil-in-the-fingernails type of people. So, it is part of my nature. This love has also been nurtured into me throughout my whole life. My parents nurtured this love in me, as did the natural world Herself. With Her beauty, surprises, power, and lessons, She has risen up to meet me in every place I have ever lived.

In Minnesota, it has been a wonder throughout my life to witness the graceful community—a waterdance—of loons as they gather on the lakes Up North. In South Dakota, the butterfly that rested on my cousin Aimee's finger at the Devil's Bathtub in the Black Hills is indelibly marked in my memory. Every time I saw a deer on my early morning drive to high school in suburban Minneapolis felt to me like a God-sighting. Lake Michigan, specifically the Dunes in Indiana, served as a way to welcome me back to college. Then, years later when I moved to Milwaukee, the Lake welcomed me again, inviting me to walk along her shores and find respite in the midst of my working, urban life. When I left Wisconsin to move back to Minnesota to attend seminary, a double rainbow greeted me to assure me that all would be well in this new beginning. Utah, my home for the past many years, introduced me to the Great Salt Lake, a unique place of desolate beauty and a visible barometer of the water crisis the West is facing.

The flatlands of Kansas and South Dakota and Southern Minnesota offered me the perspective of expansiveness and reminded me of my ability to imagine far into the distance. The mountains of Colorado, Wyoming, and Utah reminded me how small I am in the family of things. The waves of the Pacific Ocean, my backyard in Orange County, California, offered the sound of a peaceful rhythm. Trees, in every place, taught me different things in each season. To let go. To rest. To regenerate. To breathe.

The natural world has offered me regular respite and daily, ordinary invitations into contemplation and into the very heart of the Holy One my whole life. Her presence is such a part of my life that I need to be careful I do not take Her for granted. I need to remember to really look and see the color of the sky. Listen to the birdsong. Taste the sweetness of the grape tomato I grew in my garden. Feel the winter cold on my tender cheeks. Smell the leaves as they stop their work of photosynthesis, let go of their green color, and fall to the ground. The natural world hands Herself over to us in the most ordinary and right-outside-on-our-doorstep kinds of ways. And, every once in a while, She offers Herself in extraordinary ways when we cannot help but be aware that we have received a great gift, a grace beyond anything we can generate or wield on our own.

It was the summer of 2014 when I had the experience of communing with owls during a midday paddling excursion. Causey Reservoir, above the Ogden Valley, near Huntsville, Utah, is a special place to my family. We love to cliff-jump into its emerald-green waters in the late spring, meet friends to paddle board and swim on hot summer days, journey back to multi-canyon headwaters to witness the salmon spawn in the fall, and cross-country ski among the people ice fishing in winter. Of all the beautiful, connective, fun times I have had on the reservoir, the Summer Day of the Owls has been the singular best experience of all.

On this particular day, I was with my family and friends, in kayaks and canoes. We had paddled beyond the crowds where the three fingers of the reservoir meet, to quieter waters with less people. One of my favorite places on the reservoir is where a towering rock wall rises right out of the water and goes straight up for about 150 feet. Pine trees populate the rock cliff above. When my boys were little, this was the place where we would always yell "Echo!" so we could hear our own voices reflect back to us off this wall. On this particular day, as we approached the area, something different happened. Before we could call out, "Echo!" I could have sworn I heard an owl calling out "Whoo." But how could that be?

It was midafternoon on a bright, sunny day. Owls are nocturnal. Still, I hushed my boat-mates and hooted out my own best owl call. "Whoo—who-who-who-whoo." I waited. Sure enough, an owl called back from the evergreens high above us. I called again. It called again. Then, another owl called. I called. They called. And on it went. Time suspended. It truly is one of the most amazing experiences I have ever had in the natural world. Somehow, I was not simply observing. I was in communion. It did not take me long to equate this extraordinary experience as one of God's Presence.

Since this day, I have not been able to travel the reservoir in the same way. That Summer Day of the Owls offered me an experience that felt important and meaningful. I found myself striving to recreate it every chance I got. In the first couple years that followed, whenever I found myself on the water below that towering rock wall, I could not help but call out to the owls again. Every time. "Whoo—who-who-who-whoo!" I would strain my ears, hush my fellow paddlers, but the owls never called back. I was never able to re-create that moment. The owls remained silent. Over time, I could feel the joy of the initial Summer Day of the Owls get overtaken by something else. Disappointment. Disenchantment. I so desired to have that same experience of God again.

A year and a half after this Summer Day of the Owls, I entered the Spiritual Guidance Program through Shalem. The program invited me into a community of kindred spirits. It did not make me into a contemplative person but offered me the language that helped solidify and expand the spiritually contemplative way in which I wanted to continue to explore and drink in my life and the world. The teachings about the value of dropping into my heart space and how I can touch into the mystery of God from there remain important in my life of prayer and faith. The invitation to trust the *imago dei* that lives in me feels foundational in my journey of learning to love myself more deeply. It opens my eyes to see this same image of God in all of humanity, which seems essential in navigating the brokenness and division we are experiencing in our country and human global community in these days.

The training and practice around learning to be a good listener offers a great gift to people with whom I sit in spiritual direction, in part because it gives them space to speak aloud the wisdom that already exists within themselves. There are so many ways that my life as a spiritually contemplative person has been buoyed up by what I learned in my time at Shalem.

One teaching, in particular, helped me address the disappointment I was experiencing because of the silence of the owls since that one exquisite experience on the reservoir. That is, that:

> God's Presence is with us in every moment. God is revealed in all sorts of ways, from the commonplace to the miraculous. We do not get to force God or manipulate God. (In fact, we cannot.) We can only receive God as pure grace and gift.

Applying this learning to my experience with the owls eventually changed how I was able to approach that towering rock wall. I began to feel an opening. Part of that opening included getting curious. What actual continuing signs of God's Presence was I missing because I was so hyper focused on getting the owls to hoot again? As I singularly concentrated on the owls above, did I miss noticing a deer on the opposite shore coming to the reservoir for a drink of water? As I tuned my ears to hear a "hoot" above, did I miss the sound of a fish splashing below?

My curiosity expanded beyond this particular experience too. Where else in my life am I limiting God or the ways I imagine God will show up in my life or the world? Are there other situations in my life where I am content trying to create a formulaic way of experiencing God instead of allowing God to be the Wild Mystery that God is? How do I stay open and expectant enough to recognize the exceptional ways God shows up and also grounded enough in my day-to-day reality to see God in the customary ordinariness of everyday life?

As I engaged my contemplative practices and learnings over time, a shift happened. All these years later, I still call out to the owls when we reach the towering rock wall. Every single time. But I am no longer disappointed when they don't call back. My calling out "Whoo—who-who-who-whoo" is no longer an act of me trying to force the Natural World, or the owls, or God, to show up in a certain way. It is a practice of remembering. Of remembering that singular Summer Day of the Owls. It is a practice of appreciation and gratitude which are gifts unto themselves. Gratitude for the owls when they hoot and when they are silent.

Silence is an ever-persistent invitation and value I experience as I continue to seek ways of living contemplatively. The initial invitation to a practice of silence, which was such an essential aspect of Shalem's Spiritual Guidance Program, was a steep learning curve for me. It was not something I had been so intentionally invited into before. I was a trained pastor and preacher, after all. My job was to talk! To lead the congregation in communal oration of prayers and petitions. To pray with and for God's Beloveds in my care.

Learning to be with God in silence opened me up to a part of my communion and conversation with God that had been missing for far too long. God has quite a bit of love, wisdom, peace, and guidance to impart to us. The practice of getting quiet has expanded the ways in which I am able to receive all that God wants to offer.

It has taken me quite a while to come to this, but I now understand the silence of the owls in a renewed way. Being steeped in contemplative spirituality offered me a lens through which to see differently. Whereas the silence of the owls used to be disappointing, now it is illuminating. It shines a brilliant light on the uniqueness of the Summer Day of the Owls. It underscores what a gift of grace this unlikely communion with the owls was in the first place. The silence is now a source of joy that this Day ever happened at all.

Contributors

Althea Banda-Hansmann is the founding director of Transforming Moments Consulting, where she offers spiritual direction, coaching, and organizational development services. She is part of Luther Seminary's spiritual direction team in St. Paul, Minnesota, where she offers online individual and group accompaniment. Althea is a graduate of Shalem's Soul of Leadership program.

The Rev. Dr. Margaret Benefiel is Shalem's executive director. A Quaker, she is a spiritual director, teacher, retreat leader, and a graduate of Shalem's Spiritual Guidance program. She directs Shalem's Soul of Leadership program and has written extensively on various aspects of contemplative leadership and spirituality at work, including *Crisis Leadership; The Soul of Higher Education; The Soul of Supervision; The Soul of a Leader;* and *Soul at Work.*

Kolya Braun-Greiner is an interfaith educator, facilitator, and curriculum writer focused on the intersection of faith and environmental justice, encouraging people to explore their own faith tradition and finding inspiration to act for a healing and a reverent relationship with God's Creation. She is a certified Work That Reconnects facilitator.

Dr. Lerita Coleman Brown, professor emerita of psychology, spiritual director, and retreat leader, promotes contemplative spirituality and the renown mystic, Howard Thurman. She is the author of several articles, chapters, and two books, including her latest, *What Makes You Come Alive-A Spiritual Walk with Howard Thurman.*

Valerie Brown is an award-winning author, Buddhist-Quaker Dharma teacher, facilitator, and executive coach specializing in leadership development and mindfulness practices with a focus on diversity, social equity, and inclusion. Her most recent book is *Hope Leans Forward: Braving Your Way toward Simplicity, Awakening, and Peace.*

Dr. Anita-Yvonne (AY) Bryant holds a doctorate in clinical/community psychology from the University of Maryland and has served over thirty years as a psychologist, administrator, and equity advocate in higher education. She is a graduate of Shalem Institute's Soul of Leadership program and serves as a codirector of the Heart Longings: An Invitation to the Contemplative Path program.

The Rev. Dr. Gay L. Byron is professor of New Testament and Early Christianity at Howard University School of Divinity. She is the author of *Symbolic Blackness and Ethnic Difference in Early Christian Literature, Womanist Interpretations of the Bible* (coedited with Vanessa Lovelace), and *Black Scholars Matter: Visions, Struggles, and Hopes in Africana Biblical Studies* (coedited with Hugh R. Page Jr.).

The Rev. Dr. Winston Breeden Charles is a spiritual director, teacher, and poet, who as an Episcopal priest served churches for thirty-five years. Through Shalem, he discovered the rich Wisdom tradition of contemplative spirituality and was for several years director of Shalem's program for clergy, *Going Deeper: Clergy Spiritual Life and Leadership.*

The Rev. Dr. Melanie Dobson is an assistant professor and the Lefler and Wohltmann Chair in Methodist Studies at Lutheran Theological Southern Seminary (LTSS) of Lenoir-Rhyne University. She also directs the seminary's two-year Spiritual Direction Certification program. Dobson also is a registered yoga teacher and incorporates yoga into her ministry and community service.

Jackson Droney is Shalem's director of operations and online learning. Jackson is a graduate of Shalem's Personal Spiritual Deepening program, Young Adult Life and Leadership Initiative, and Soul of Leadership program. He is a student at Luther Seminary and is a candidate for pastoral ministry in the Evangelical Lutheran Church in America (ELCA).

Sarah Forti is a contemplative ministry leader, songwriter, and fencer. She has a BA in religious studies from Virginia Commonwealth University, an MDiv from George Fox Evangelical Seminary, and is a graduate of the Shalem Institute. Sarah resides in Ashland, Virginia, with her husband, Nik, and their son, Thomas.

Amanda Lindamood is a postpartum doula, organizational consultant, creative educator, and freelance writer with multidisciplinary experience and training. She brings to contemplative leadership a commitment to Black feminisms, womanism, spiritual depth, community organizing and children's liberation, and lived and professional experience in complex trauma.

Marcelle Martin has led workshops across the United States and was a resident teacher at Pendle Hill. She is the author of *Our Life is Love: The Quaker Spiritual Journey, A Guide to Faithfulness Groups*, and the blog *A Whole Heart*. Swarthmore Friends Meeting supports her ministry of spiritual nurture.

Dr. Westina Matthews is an author, retreat leader, spiritual director, and workshop facilitator who has found a way to connect with others through her writings, speaking, and teaching. A graduate of Shalem Institute's Spiritual Guidance program, she currently serves on the Shalem board. Her latest book is *This Band of Sisterhood*.

Carl McColman is a graduate of Shalem's Personal Spiritual Deepening program (1986) and Leading Contemplative Groups program (1987), a popular contemplative blogger, podcast host (Encountering Silence), and author of books, including *The New Big Book of Christian Mysticism, Unteachable Lessons*, and *Eternal Heart*.

Dr. Leah Moran Rampy is a Shalem graduate who has served as board member, executive director, program leader, and pilgrimage guide. Founder of *Church of the Wild Two Rivers*, she leads retreats and writes about the call to reweave Earth and soul. Leah and her husband, David, live in Shepherdstown, West Virginia.

Rev. DanaLee Simon, a Lutheran pastor and spiritual director, lives with her husband and two sons in Salt Lake City, Utah. When she's not out communing in Nature, she can be found teaching self-compassion, connecting with people in spiritual direction, writing, or driving a carpool.

J. M. Smith lives in Washington, D.C. and enjoys writing at the intersections of social justice and contemplative life.

Phillip Stephens is the director of Nurturing the Call, Shalem Institute's Spiritual Guidance program. He is an Episcopal layperson and graduate of the 2006 Spiritual Guidance Class. In addition to being an associate of the Order of the Holy Cross, he serves as a spiritual guide and retreat facilitator. His interests include cross-cultural studies and interspirituality.

Elaine Voci is a life coach, grief group facilitator, and the author of *Bridge Builders: Ordinary Women Doing Extraordinary Things* and *Creating the Work You Love: A Guide to Finding Your Right Livelihood*. She lives in the Midwest with her spouse.

Joanne Youn is a published author and speaker with a passion for collaboration among diverse demographics both within the United States and abroad. Although she has lived and served in various locations around the world, she currently resides with her husband, Tom, and their three children outside of Washington, DC.

Vision Statement 2025

Our hearts leapt when we encountered Shalem—we were changed. For Margaret this happened in the 1980s, for Jackson in the 2010s. Both of us encountered a space and community that was hungry for God, eager to listen to the Holy, and desiring spaciousness and authenticity in our individual and shared response. We felt God's transforming and loving presence, and an invitation to the contemplative path that has profoundly shaped our lives. For us and for many, it was a sense of coming home.

This sense of coming home is not passive. It's an active, ongoing pilgrim journey with God and community that cultivates an inner life that nourishes us to be bearers and sharers of the Great Love. At its best, this is what Shalem offers each of us: the opportunity to grow in love with one another for the sake of the world. The Holy One guides and leads this activity, and we're continually invited to step into that flow. This sacred space and precious calling make the vitality of Shalem deeply important to us, and we know it does the same for many of you too.

In 2020 the whole world seemed to enter a communal dark night of the soul. Political divisions in our country, the coronavirus pandemic, and racial injustice roiled us. We took this situation to prayer: What does this all mean for our lives? What does this all mean for our world? What does this mean for Shalem?

Around this time, we noticed that the items described in the Shalem 2018 strategic plan were mostly completed. We sensed the growing importance of Shalem's mission to nurture contemplative life and leadership. Indeed, to be present to the world in this communal dark night and to grow in organizational health, we sensed a holy invitation to discern a vision for Shalem's future, a prophetic call that invites us to grow deeper in faith both internally and in our witness to the world.

This discernment process began at the staff-board retreat in March 2021 and continued with the formation of a vision coalition made up of board members, office staff, and program staff. We are grateful for the faithful service of that group: Sallie Chatfield, Susan Etherton, Katy Gaughan, Laura Neal, Lisa Senuta, Phillip Stephens, Nan Weir, Sarah Willie-LeBreton, and along with the two of us. We shared our experiences of Shalem, noticed patterns in Shalem's history, discussed our dreams for Shalem's future, and listened to reflections of the board and hundreds of others who participated in ten (yes, ten!) listening sessions.

This discernment led to the drafting of a vision statement, guiding principles, and focus areas.

- The vision statement articulates what we hear the Holy inviting Shalem to become in 2025.
- The guiding principles describe who we are and what we commit to for that vision to manifest.
- And the focus areas offer practical direction for our organizational life so that our vision can come alive.

The board approved this vision at its meeting on November 11, 2022, and it is with both humility and confidence that we present it to you now.

Margaret Benefiel and Jackson Droney

VISION 2025: OUR ONGOING HOPE

Imagining the future and mindful of the challenges of our times, Shalem is grateful to commence its next chapter embracing opportunities for renewed vision and vitality.

Our faithful work continues with eyes and hearts open to see the greater impact Shalem might have on our hurting world. Our grief and response to the pandemic, racial injustice, political unrest, and the climate crisis has drawn us again to the ancient longing for wholeness and oneness in the Spirit.

With a greater number of people participating in Shalem programs, a new awareness of necessary organizational changes has surfaced. To sense the movement of the Spirit, a Vision Coalition was created and invited to listen to our broad community. Deep prayer and active listening led to drafting a Vision Statement, Guiding Principles, and Focus Areas to guide us as we respond to God's lifegiving activity. this is Vision 2025.

As Vision 2025 propels us into this next chapter, we invite you to imagine the power and possibility of our collective contemplative discernment and compassion. We invite your bold prayers and courageous hope.

Mission Statement:

To nurture contemplative living and leadership

Vision Statement:

In 2025, Shalem will be a dynamic and inclusive community, empowered by the Spirit, where seekers engage in transformation of themselves, their communities, and the world through spiritual growth, deep connection, and courageous action.

Guiding Principles:

- Responding to Divine Initiative, we allow the Divine to lead us into shared practices of sacred stillness, deep listening, open-heartedness, and prayer.
- With Holy Awe, we will practice cultivating gratitude, curiosity, joy, and delight, celebrating the power of Love to transform.
- We acknowledge the uniqueness of each spiritual path and welcome the creative possibilities our gifts and experience bring to Shalem and the world.
- Grounded in the Christian contemplative tradition, we will celebrate the diversity of all contemplative traditions and lift up the voices beyond historically dominant ones.
- As beloved community, we will face our fears and act with compassion and courage to challenge injustice, dismantle systems of inequity, and pursue reconciliation.
- We affirm Sacred Abundance within and around us and will seek to act with generosity and trustworthiness as we steward our resources—human, natural, and financial.

Focus Areas:

Contemplative Grounding

Contemplative grounding is our expression of the Great Love at the center of all things. As we continue to be drawn to the edge of God's longing, we are invited to a fresh articulation of that expression (Deut. 6:4–9).

Belonging

Belonging is the manifestation of God's union with all things. When we are radically inclusive, we embrace the Loving Essence of each individual. A sense of belonging for each of us follows as we are part of something larger than ourselves while honoring who we are and who we want to be (John 17:21–23).

Capacity Building

Capacity building is not a one-time effort to improve short-term effectiveness; it is the intentional and continuous imagining of what is needed for Shalem to grow to the next level of operational, programmatic, financial, and organizational maturity so that we may more effectively and faithfully live our mission into the future (Luke 14:28–30, Jer. 29:11–13).

Sustainability

Sustainability occurs when we attract and effectively use enough and the right kind of resources to achieve our long-term goals. Sustainability invites us to prayerfully consider the whys and ways we invite, receive, and utilize our resources (1 Peter 4:10).

Generating

Generating is action fueled by courage, confidence, and hope. Embracing mystery, we seek to discover new ways of expressing the contemplative Christian tradition beyond the usual exchange of information (Jer. 6:16).

Portions of this essay first appeared as "Introducing Vision 2025: Our Ongoing Hope" in Shalem Institute Friday Blog (January 27, 2023). Used with permission.

Acknowledgments

W e are filled with deep gratitude for everyone who submitted essays for this book and continued to lift up prayers as we discerned the final selection of essays. It was on the wings of prayers of the larger Shalem community that we labored over the past year to bring this book to fruition, and for that we give thanks.

We offer a special thank you to Airié Stuart, publisher of Church Publishing Inc., who understood the vision for this book; and to our editor, Eve Strillacci, who honored the voices of our individual contributors as she thoughtfully suggested revisions. Valerie Brown immediately agreed to contribute the foreword to the book, and for this we add our heartful thank you. There also are those who either quietly offered guidance on how to shape the book, or provided another pair of eyes for copy editing, or who assisted in their own quiet ways: Fay Acker, Alfonso Campbell III, Susan Etherton, Carolyn Green, Joan Loos, Anne Mallonee, Patience Robbins, Anne Silver, David Wantland, and Sarah Willie-LeBreton.

Our cup overflows in thanksgiving for being awarded a grant from Trinity Church Wall Street to support Shalem's Diversity, Equity, and Inclusion initiatives—of which *Soul Food* is a part. With this grant, we are grateful to be able to provide honorariums for each of the contributors. We, the editors, will also direct all our royalties from this book to the Shalem Institute in support of its vision to become a dynamic and inclusive community. Thank you for your "holy yes" to this important work.

Printed in the USA
CPSIA information can be obtained
at www.ICGtesting.com
JSHW051120110923
48253JS00004B/23